GLORY

OF THE

GAMES

Chad Bonham

GLORY OF THE GAMES

Cross Training Publishing
www.crosstrainingpublishing.com
(308) 293-3891

Copyright © 2012 by Chad Bonham
ISBN: 978-1-938254-02-4

Portions of the content taken from interviews with Chris Byrd, Tamika Catchings, Michael Chang, Josh Davis, Jarome Iginla, Bobby Jones and Laura Wilkinson copyright Fellowship of Christian Athletes, used by permission.

Photo Credits
Chris Byrd cover photo courtesy of Chris and Tracy Byrd
Shannon Miller cover photo by Dave Black
Hunter Kemper cover photo by Dan Apol
Josh Davis cover photo courtesy of Josh Davis
Tamika Catchings cover photo courtesy of USA Basketball Photos
Ryan Hall cover photo by Noor Noordin
(www.flickr.com/photos/innusa)
Shannon Miller back cover photo by Mike Proebsting

Acknowledgements

I'd like to publicly thank the Lord for blessing me with the skill and desire to be in this wonderful position as a published author. I'm incredibly grateful for the opportunities He has afforded me to impact others with His empowering, inspiring and life-changing Gospel message.

I also can't express enough love and appreciation for my wife Amy and my amazing three boys Lance, Cole and Quinn (and even Jack, our golden retriever who kept me company on those rare occasions when I had time by myself at the house). They fuel my fire and help me push through the most challenging aspects of being a writer. Along with them, I want to thank my mother Betty Bonham for her constant prayers and words of encouragement, and my sisters Rhonda Dilldine and Karla Partridge (and their awesome families) for the years of undying support.

Thanks to Gordon Thiessen who caught the vision for this project and allowed me the chance to share it with a larger audience through Cross Training Publishing. When we first connected I had no idea how many fantastic concepts would come from a new friendship. I'm looking forward to what the future holds.

Thanks also go to the amazing individuals featured in this book. I've been blessed to get to know them all (as well as many of their associates) through various phone conversations, email correspondences and face-to-face meetings: Chris Byrd, Tracy Byrd; Tamika Catchings; Michael Chang, Caroline Wong Nakata, Chang Family Foundation; Kelly Clark, Elise Alderson; Josh Davis; Kevin Durant, Brian Davis, Brian Facchini, the Oklahoma City Thunder; Ryan Hall; Tobin Heath, John Archibald, Sky Blue FC; Chad

Hedrick; Jarome Iginla, Peter Hanlon, the Calgary Flames; Dave Johnson, Elisa Schwarze, Corban University Athletic Department; Bobby Jones; DeLisha Milton-Jones, Ben Alkaly, the Los Angeles Sparks; Hunter Kemper; Shannon Miller, Lauren Domené; Ruth Riley; Lyndon Rush, Chris Dornan, High-Performance Public Relations; Laura Wilkinson; Pat Williams, Andrew Herdliska; Jane Albright; Mike Jarvis; and Ron Thulin.

I'd also like thank some other great folks who were instrumental in helping this project happen in one way or another: Jill Ewert, Dan Britton, Shea Vailes, Fellowship of Christian Athletes, Sharing the Victory Magazine; Brett Honeycutt, Sports Spectrum; Jimmy Stewart, Adrienne Gaines, Strang Communications; Caroline Williams, USA Basketball; Noor Nordin.

And finally, special thanks go to Tulsa Hardesty Library for providing a quiet, resourceful place to research and write, as well as Panera Bread Co. (various franchises in Broken Arrow and Tulsa, Okla.) for free wireless internet, endless trips to the beverage dispenser and great sandwiches, salads and pastries. Now, if we could just find a way to put all of those things together in one convenient location.

Preface

According to the Bible, God designed each of us to reflect the moral nature of God Himself. For that reason, the character traits demonstrated by the athletes in this book are closely related—the fruit of God's grace.

Glory of the Games includes eighteen Olympic athletes that demonstrate positive moral character. Anyone can benefit from their approach to building Christ-like character and learning how to better glorify the Lord in all areas of life.

The author calls us as Christians to turn from pride and self-centeredness and study the character of Christ to be filled with grace. We need to be careful not to simply teach ourselves moral lessons and put teaching character traits ahead of the main focus, which is the gospel: God sent His Son to the cross to bear His wrath for sinners like you and me. Don't allow this or any other study on character to become just good advice rather than good news.

Jerry Bridges writes, "This gospel is not only the most important message in all of history; it is the only essential message in all of history. Yet we allow thousands of professing Christians to live their entire lives without clearly understanding it and experiencing the joy of living by it."

While I have spent most of my life serving in ministry through the Fellowship of Christian Athletes, Christian education and the local church ministry, there was a time that Christianity was not part of my life. During college, several friends told me that on the cross Jesus took my place, that he took every one of my sins upon himself and was resurrected from the dead three days later. Late one night, the incredible implications of the Son of God dying in my place for my sin overwhelmed my soul. I rejoiced in the truth. That night I repented of my sin and placed my faith and trust in Jesus Christ. The awesome work of Jesus that brought me to life and made me God's son is the same power that can save you.

Once I realized that I deserved the full wrath or anger of God because of my sin, the good news that God loved me enough to provide a way to be saved changed my life. My life has never been the same since that night in college. And one day, when Jesus returns, I will receive a glorified body. I will rise with him, and my weak body will be transformed. His great and mighty salvation will be complete.

Christians often say that Jesus died for our sins. But what does that mean? Why did he die? What has he accomplished by this death on the cross? What effect does his death on a cross have on us? What does it change? In order to understand the gospel, we need to understand the facts behind it. Below are the facts I share about God whenever I have the chance to talk about the Gospel. Gospel Facts:

> That the one and only one God, who is holy, made us in his image to know him. However, we have sinned and cut ourselves off from him. Because of God's love for us, God became a man in Jesus, lived a perfect life, and died on the cross. He fulfilled the law himself by taking on the punishment we deserved for the sins of all those who ever turn to and trust him. He rose again from the dead, showing that God accepted Christ's sacrifice and that God's wrath against us had been exhausted. Now, God calls us to repent of our sins and trust in Christ, we are born again into a new life, an eternal life with God.

The Apostle Paul points to the gospel as the one thing that should motivate all our work and affect every part of our character. Paul taught "For I delivered to you as of first importance what I also received: that Christ died for our sins, in accordance with the Scriptures, that he was buried, that he was raised on the third day in accordance with the Scriptures...." 1 Corinthians 15:3-4

I remember reading something else Bridges wrote years ago. "Preach the gospel to ourselves every day." Since that time, I have tried to make this a daily practice of my life and in my ministry.

Let me encourage you to remind yourself that the gospel is more than a door we walk through to become a Christian. The gospel is not only for the lost but also for the found. The cross and its meaning aren't something that we ever master. David Prior said, "We never move on from the cross, only to a more profound understanding of the cross."

I hope you will find this book both interesting and helpful to your Christian life. May you always see Christ's character and desire to see it reproduced in your own life, and may pursuing Godly character produce in you a more profound understanding of the cross.

Gordon Thiessen, Publisher

Foreword

When I was just beginning my running career, as a 14-year-old kid in Big Bear Lake, Ca, I would frequently daydream about the Olympics. I remember wondering what Olympians were like. I never knew an Olympian personally, which led me to be curious about their personalities. I always imagined them to be grounded, nearly perfect people. I couldn't have been more wrong.

Fifteen years later, after recently qualifying for my second Olympic Team in the marathon, I realize that one of the biggest characteristics that has led to my success has not been that I never fail (in fact there have been many more failures that successes) but that I have learned to get back up after stumbling. I have learned the principle of endurance. It's not that I never get knocked down but that I always, by the grace of God, find the strength in Christ to get back up. My character has gotten stronger and stronger as God has taught me how to rise again. One of the verses in the Bible that I think best describes myself and most successful people comes from Proverbs 24:16. "For a righteous man falls seven times, and rises again."

Now, it is my goal to share what I have learned to the generations to come so that they don't have to make the same mistakes I made. This book will be a treasure for those looking to gain valuable insights into the lives of those who have been through all the seasons of life and come out the other side. I pray that this book blesses you and imparts to you the ability to realize your full God-given potential in the gifts God has given you.

-Ryan Hall
Co-founder of a growing community of radical
runners stepping together to end global poverty.
www.thestepsfoundation.org.

Introduction

I've always had a curious fascination with the Olympic Games. Perhaps it was the pageantry that first caught my eye as a nine-year old growing up in Northeastern Oklahoma. I loved flags when I was kid (still do), so watching the teams march into a stadium behind their nations' colors was an incredible sight.

Of course, part of the appeal was rooting on Team USA in every sport imaginable. It didn't matter if it was summer or winter, boxing or the biathlon, field hockey or figure skating, canoeing or curling. If it was in the Olympics, I was interested. So much so that I often tracked the daily medal counts and wrote them down in a notebook. I had to rely on the newspaper since the Internet was still nothing more than a science fiction fantasy at the time.

My earliest memory of the Olympics was the 1980 Winter Games in Lake Placid. I especially recall Eric Heiden's speed skating performance on the outdoor rink that yielded five gold medals. And who doesn't remember the Miracle on Ice when the out-matched US team defeated the vaunted USSR squad en route to the historic gold?

I laugh when I remember how later that summer I was literally angry with President Jimmy Carter for boycotting the Summer Games in Moscow amid growing tensions between the United State and the Communist Soviet Union. Of course, I had little understanding of geopolitics and was merely disappointed for the American athletes who would miss their opportunity to participate in the greatest sports event on the planet.

When the 1984 Summer Games in Los Angeles took place, I was excited for the opportunity to watch the event in real time thanks to the broadcast-friendly time zone. The competition lacked many Eastern European countries that boycotted in response to the American boycott four years earlier. But the Games were star-studded nonetheless. Carl Lewis, Mary Lou Retton, Edwin Moses, Florence Griffith, Greg Louganis, Michael Jordan and Evander Holyfield represented a ridiculous amount of talent for the dominant home team.

At that point in my life, there was no way to know that I would eventually have a chance to interview, write about and even become friends with numerous Olympians. I've been blessed to meet many well-known athletes and entertainers, but I get especially excited about talking to people who have risen to the highest level of international competition. There is something special about the Olympic athlete.

And therein lies some big questions. What makes the Olympic athlete special? What does it take to become an Olympic athlete? One thing I've learned in talking to these people is that there are several characteristics that can usually be found operating in their lives—attributes such as determination, endurance, focus, integrity, passion, patience and self-discipline.

But the ones that have always stood out to me the most are those that understand the true purpose behind their athletic success. These Olympians have come to realize that they have been blessed with athleticism and drive in order to bring glory to God and share with others the hope that accompanies a relationship with Jesus Christ. And that's when a new set of values begins to shine—qualities such as humility, service, faithfulness and spiritual maturity.

In the pages that follow, you will read about 18 Olympic

athletes who have achieved amazing things and reaped the benefits of their success. But what you'll also find is a group of men and women who are striving for a greater purpose. That purpose is to offer the God they serve the *Glory of the Games*. — Chad Bonham

Contents

CHAPTER ONE

Trust God's Plan
Featuring Dave Johnson, USA
Olympic Bronze Medalist, Decathlon

The best laid schemes of mice and men
Go often askew[1]

Dave Johnson is one man who can relate to the truth behind that famous line in the Robert Burns poem "To A Mouse." Johnson had a plan. It was a good plan. After finishing ninth at the 1988 Summer Olympics in Seoul, the decathlete from the Great Northwest continued to rise as one of the sport's dominant forces. He won gold at the 1989 World University Games in Duisburg, Germany and set an American record that same year at the U.S. Track and Field Championships. The 1992 Summer Games in Barcelona were his for the taking.

This was his time.

"In my mind, I thought that the Lord had a perfect thing for me and that it was going to be a gold medal and a world record," Johnson says. "Once I started to feel His strength and I started to think about the possibilities, there was nothing that could stop me. Win a gold medal and be there to shine for the Lord. That was the goal."[2]

But in 1991, newcomer Dan O'Brien hit the scene and proceeded to shake things up. He won the World Championships in Tokyo that year and set a world record of 8,891 points in the months leading up to the '92 Olympics. Reebok featured the two athletes in its pervasive "Dan & Dave" television commercials. Johnson wasn't worried about O'Brien's skyrocketing success, but in fact welcomed the emergence of a new rival.

"I rejoiced when Dan came around," Johnson says. "It was nice. It was local. It was in the United States. It was one of those things that I saw the Lord bringing into the situation. I knew it was what He wanted. At the time, I was always first or second in the world and now there was a major company wanting to push me into the public eye through this multi-media advertising campaign. I knew that it was the Lord doing that."[3]

But at the 1992 U.S. Olympic Trials, things started to go "askew," as Robert Burns might say. O'Brien decided not to attempt the easier heights in the pole vault but then failed to score a clean jump as the bar was raised higher. That proved fatal to his overall score and he shockingly did not qualify for the Olympic team.

"The hype was based around both of us going to the Olympic games and then he didn't make the team," Johnson recalls. "I was thinking, 'Great, why did that happen?'"[4]

Johnson was having his own problems at the time. Leading up to the Trials, he had injured his right foot, but not severely enough to keep him from competing and qualifying for the U.S. team.[5] After his final event, Johnson limped off the field after aggravating the previous bruising. Fortunately for Johnson, he had been training at Azusa Pacific University with a group of Christian athletes who helped keep him focused on God and His purpose.[6]

But even the spiritual growth experienced through that fellowship of accountability was put to the test once Johnson took the field of competition in Barcelona. After the first five events, he was in ninth place with 4,154 points. By no means was he out of medal contention. As the world record holder in second day points, Johnson knew there was ample opportunity for making up ground on his opponents. Instead, the bigger issue was his nagging foot injury that was no longer just a severe bruise. X-rays revealed that Johnson now had a stress fracture. The elite athlete did his best to stay positive, but he found it difficult to find the silver lining in the dark cloud that was camped out over his head.

"Part of me was saying, 'Man, Lord, you messed this up,'" Johnson candidly admits.[7]

Johnson fought through the pain but faced an especially challenging moment in the pole vault. By then, his foot was swollen and running at any modest pace was nearly impossible. Johnson knew that he would need to generate enough speed to keep the pole from bending. What would usually be a routine task had suddenly become overwhelmingly difficult.

"Just before my first attempt, I went into prayer," Johnson recounts. "'Lord, I can't warm up. I'm on my smallest pole. I don't think I can get on this thing. The bar is at 15 feet. I should be able to make that easily, but why now? Why are we doing this now?' I was almost in tears."[8]

At that moment, Johnson leaned on God's capable arms and the many prayers that were going up on his behalf. And then, a very powerful visual enveloped his mind and provided the strength and inspiration he desperately needed.

"I saw Christ carrying the cross," Johnson says. "He picked it up like a vaulting pole and He was running with it. Even after being whipped and bloodied, He was still running. And then he stuck the cross into a hole in the ground and jumped up onto it. Through this prayer, it just hit me. He specifically died for each and every one of us."[9]

Johnson had heard the chatter around the stadium and in the press. He knew that everyone expected him to fail that day. But through his vision of Jesus' sacrifice on the cross, Johnson felt like the Lord was telling him, "Give your life to me. Don't believe those things. I'm going to take care of it."[10]

Johnson miraculously made the height and finished the event with enough points to move up in the field. He didn't have his best overall performance by a long shot, but a score of 8,309 points put him in position to win the bronze medal. It was a triumphant moment that in some ways turned out to be more inspirational than capturing a gold medal injury-free. Even still, Johnson has often wondered what might have been.

"I realized the level of where it was going," Johnson says. "It would have needed the gold medal and a world record, but there were things waiting to happen that would have been amazing. I was confident that I would have reflected the Lord doing those things, but He had something else planned for my life instead. I've always been able to remind myself that I wasn't there for all of those big things. I was there to allow the Lord to work through me and use me for whatever He wanted."[11]

Johnson retired from competition in 1998 and went on to finish his master's in special education. He taught seven years before earning his administrative credentials in 2005. After serving as an athletic director and vice principal at two high schools in Oregon, Johnson took the next logical step and joined the administration at Corbin University in Salem as the NAIA program's athletic director. It wasn't what Johnson planned for back in his competitive glory days, but he can't see his life any differently.

"Through my years as a high school teacher and a high school track coach, it's allowed me to be in a kid's life and understand that they have a lot going on and they just need someone to listen to them," Johnson says. "They needed someone to be their mentor and their example of how to get out of the mess they might be in. It's taught me to be available for kids and students. Now that I'm at a university, I get to be in these athletes' lives and help them see their potential. These kids can do anything if we help them and lead them to that relationship with Christ. In the end, that's what my life experiences were all for, so I could be in a student's life and be a positive role model."[12]

Trusting God's plan for our lives would probably be a lot easier if we knew the end result in advance. It's a much trickier proposition when we look at things from a human perspective. Just like Johnson, we often base God's plan on what we see with the natural eye—our circumstances, our opportunities, our talents and our personal views of what we deem is best for us.

But that's not how God works. He wants us to trust Him. He wants us to wholeheartedly believe that He always has our best interest at the forefront of His will. In Proverbs 3:5-6, King Solomon advises the reader to, "Trust in the LORD with all your heart, and do not rely on your own understanding; think about Him in all your ways, and He will guide you on the right paths."

The Old Testament story of the Israelites shows us what happens when people trust God and what happens when they take matters into their own hands. After being rescued from captivity in Egypt, it didn't take long for the Israelites to forget the awesome displays of God's power. They cried out to their leader Moses thinking they had been freed, only to die at the edge of the Red Sea.

Of course, God was still faithful and parted the waters so His people could escape Pharaoh's army. (Exodus 14:1-29)

Over time, the people's disbelief, incessant complaining and rebellious ways angered God. In Numbers 14:22-23, He declared that, "none of the men who have seen my glory and my signs that I did in Egypt and in the wilderness, and yet have put me to the test these ten times and have not obeyed my voice, shall see the land that I swore to give to their fathers. And none of those who despised me shall see it." The people then proceeded to wander in the wilderness for the next 40 years. (Numbers 14:31-35)

In sharp contrast, we see the descendants of those people taking a much different approach to some unusual plans that God gave Moses' successor. When the Israelites came to the city of Jericho, tall, fortified walls stood between the people and the Promised Land. The Lord, however, told Joshua that Jericho had already been delivered into his hands. But first, the Children of Israel would need to follow some very specific instructions:

"March around the city once with all the armed men. Do this for six days. Have seven priests carry trumpets of rams' horns in front of the ark. On the seventh day, march around the city seven times, with the priests blowing the trumpets. When you hear them sound a long blast on the trumpets, have the whole army give a loud shout; then the wall of the city will collapse and the army will go up, everyone straight in." (Joshua 6:3-5)

It must have seemed crazy at the time, but the people had seen their God do seemingly crazy things before. Therefore, they trusted Joshua's instructions and followed the plan without complaint or deviation. That's when God again proved to be faithful. According to Joshua 6:20, "When the trumpets sounded, the army shouted, and at the sound of the trumpet, when the men gave a loud shout, the wall collapsed; so everyone charged straight in, and they took the city."

God's plans aren't always going to make sense. Many times, we won't know the final destination of the path He's laid before us until we've arrived. Throughout those experiences, it's best to remember His own explanation found in Isaiah 55:8. "For My thoughts are not your thoughts, and your ways are not My ways," God reminds us.

When our plans fizzle out or completely blow up in our faces, the closing line from "To A Mouse" might ring all too familiar. According to Burns, the failure of manmade schemes results in "nothing but grief and pain."[13] But when we follow God's plan, we can trust that His ways are perfect and according to Jeremiah 29:11 will give us "a future and a hope."

Johnson is one man who can certainly attest to that truth.

"I look back at my experience and I rejoice," Johnson says. "It was obvious that the Lord stepped in and was the strength behind it all. It had nothing to do with 'Dan & Dave' or Reebok or a gold medal or the world record. It was all about doing the best I could for Him. It was a golden performance to Jesus Christ."[14]

The Extra Mile

1. What are some plans that you've made that didn't work out? Were you disappointed or did you realize it was for the best?

2. Have you ever had your plans work out but were left feeling unsatisfied as a result? If so, why do you think that happened?

3. What do you think it means to completely trust in God's plan for your life? Can you think of a time when you've been able to do that? How did that journey end?

4. In Isaiah 55:8, we learn that God's thoughts and ways are much different than ours. Can you think of some examples of how God thinks and operates differently than us?

5. What are some things that you struggle to trust God for in your life? How can truly believing Jeremiah 29:11 help you to start trusting God more?

Find more of what the Bible says about trusting God's plan by reading these passages: Psalm 138:8, Proverbs 16:9, Jeremiah 29:11, Ephesians 2:10, 1 Thessalonians 5:18, James 4:13-15

CHAPTER TWO

Keep a Steady Pace
Featuring Hunter Kemper, USA
Olympic Athlete, Triathlon

When the International Olympic Committee announced that it was adding the triathlon for the 2000 Sydney Games, no one was more excited than Hunter Kemper. Unlike many tri-athletes who gravitate to the sport later in their competitive lives, Kemper had been participating in the grueling three-event race since he was just 10 years old.

"I was ecstatic," Kemper recalls. "When I was a kid growing up, I loved the Olympic Games. I had a great deal of respect for a lot of Olympic athletes—Rowdy Gaines and Matt Biondi in swimming, Michael Johnson in track and field. I loved those guys."

Before there was a triathlon event to shoot for, Kemper focused on fulfilling his Olympic dream through running. He quickly found out, however, that he wasn't quite talented enough to reach such an elite level. So Kemper abandoned that goal and put all of his energy on becoming a professional tri-athlete. He walked on at Wake Forest to improve his running and eventually turned what was a weakness into one of his strengths. But the IOC announcement changed everything.

"When they announced it would be in the Olympics, it was a whole new ball game," Kemper says. "It was a literal jump for joy and a warming of the heart to think maybe that was my path. I love the Olympics and what they stand for and what they mean. It's every four years and you have to be your best on that one day."

For Kemper, patience has been one of his keys to long-term success. He has learned over time that the triathlon is a sport where the athlete gets better with age. The raw talent and speed might provide somewhat of an advantage for younger racers, but the older, more experienced competitors can often rely on proven techniques and unique strategies to even the playing field.

That has certainly proven true over Kemper's career. He took silver at the 1999 Pan American Games in Winnipeg and then bettered that result with a gold medal performance at the 2003 Pan American Games in Santo Domingo. Kemper eventually rose to the top of the world rankings and secured several major race victories along the way. He had a banner year in 2005 when he won five races including the Escape From Alcatraz Triathlon in San Francisco and the Lifetime Fitness Triathlon in Minneapolis, which at the time paid the largest professional prize purse. Kemper also became the first American to finish the season ranked #1 in the International Triathlon Union (ITU) World Cup Series. That same year, he was named United States Olympic Committee (USOC) Sportsman of the Year.

His Olympic experience has likewise been a test of long-term patience. Kemper was 24 years old at the Sydney Games, where his 17th-place finish was the best among fellow Americans. Four years later in Athens, Kemper went into the race ranked in the top five but finished a disappointing ninth. He entered the 2008 Beijing Games with a renewed sense of purpose but a nagging injury impeded his progress. Still, he improved his career Olympic results and managed a satisfying seventh place finish, just 40 seconds off the pace from the medal stand.

"I dealt with a sports hernia going into Beijing and I wasn't at my peak performance," Kemper says. "I wasn't at my best in my training. I had to get local cortisone injections to compete in those Games. Finishing seventh was like winning a gold medal. I gave it all I had and I was happy with my performance."

Patience is equally necessary within the course of a race. In less than two hours, elite tri-athletes swim 1.5 kilometers (0.93 miles), ride a bike 40 kilometers (24.8 miles) and run 10 kilometers (6.2 miles). Kemper says it's the swimming portion of the race that often requires the greatest measure of patience.

"When we start out the race, there are 50 guys on the Olympic starting line or 75 during a World Cup event," he explains. "We're all on a pontoon diving into a body of water and there's a buoy about 300 meters out. As you go around that turn buoy, you want to be on the inside line. Everyone is sprinting for that turn buoy. It's not normal sprinting that you'd see in a pool. It's a cluster. You're getting pounded. You're getting physically beat up in the water. It's hard to see. There are no lanes. Guys are on top of you, kicking you, pushing you under. It's very physical. You have to rely on patience knowing that in that moment everyone is going through the same thing. Everyone is getting beat up. You have to remember that there's so much of the race left to be raced."

Other opportunities for patience present themselves throughout the bike riding and running segments as well. Kemper says that so often the race will come down to the final 10 kilometers or the last 30 minutes of the race. "You have to trust your game plan and stick to it," he says. "Things are going to get better when you stay patient."

Kemper has always valued the need for patience as a competitor, but it wasn't until late in his college career at Wake Forest and shortly thereafter that he started to understand the biblical significance of the principle. He had grown up attending a Presbyterian church but sports eventually took precedent over spiritual matters. "I totally lost my way and I didn't have that foundation," Kemper says.

In college, he began gravitating towards his Christian friends. He began asking himself some deep, internal questions. Kemper also started attending church more regularly and became even more committed to that practice when he moved to Colorado Springs, Colorado, for training. It was one particular service at Rocky Mountain Calvary Chapel that finally opened his heart.

"I went home after a sermon and I just broke down," Kemper says. "In the quietness of my little rental house, I wept by myself and realized I couldn't do it on my own anymore. It was a freeing feeling for me. My life has changed."

A year later, in 2000, Kemper met his wife Val, who was cut from the U.S. Volleyball team the same day of their first date. They married in 2003 and now have three young boys. Kemper's wife came from a Christian Reform Church background in Grand Rapids, Mich. and has been a vital part of her husband's spiritual growth.

Kemper is not naturally patient. Not many humans are. In fact, patience is one of the most unnatural attributes that we can attempt to attain. We want what we want, and we want it now. Often that leads to a frustrating relationship with God. We pray for the things we want and sometimes things that we truly need like financial provision, good health, timely answers to difficult questions, or help for loved ones.

David wrote about patience quite a bit in the Psalms. "Be

silent before the LORD and wait expectantly for Him," he advised. "Do not be agitated by one who prospers in his way, by the man who carries out evil plans." (Psalm 37:7) There are three key things to point out in this passage. First of all, we need to listen to what He might be trying to tell us through our difficult circumstance. Secondly, we should have the faith to believe that He will answer and He will give you what you need—not necessarily what you want, because sometimes those things aren't the same.

The last part of that verse is equally difficult to follow. We are often "agitated" or distracted when we see people around us seemingly getting what they want or having their prayers answered. It becomes especially annoying when people who don't even profess a relationship with God and don't care much about biblically sound living are prospering and getting ahead in life. That kind of attitude will kill our patience in a heartbeat and will skew our perspective of God and His sovereign ways.

It's also important to be patient with yourself. Whether it's running a race, working on an education, learning a new skill or studying God's Word and striving towards spiritual maturity, there's always a temptation hanging around our heads to give up when things don't happen quickly. Impatience inherently hinders endurance, but Isaiah 40:31 paints a beautiful picture of what happens when we lean upon Him, keep up a steady pace and resist the urge to quit:

> But those who wait on the LORD Shall renew
> *their* strength; They shall mount up with wings like
> eagles, They shall run and not be weary,
> They shall walk and not faint. (NKJV)

"When that verse talks about wings of eagles, it so pic-turesque as runner," Kemper says. "I think about that throughout the entire process. That's where I'm getting my strength. I'm at my best when I'm racing and thinking about the Lord and how He is the source of my strength."

And sometimes, perhaps most of the time even, we are faced with situations that require an enormous amount of patience with those around us. This could be true for family, friends, co-workers, teammates, fellow competitors, neighbors or people we randomly run across on a daily basis. Kemper says the Bible verse that speaks most clearly to him on the subject is found in Colossians 3:12-14.

"Therefore, God's chosen ones, holy and loved, put on heart-felt compassion, kindness, humility, gentleness, and patience, accepting one another and forgiving one another if anyone has a complaint against another. Just as the Lord has forgiven you, so you must also forgive. Above all, put on love—the perfect bond of unity."

That last word, "unity," underscores one of God's purposes behind the challenging principle of patience. In His infinite wisdom, He knows that true patience will bear incredible fruit when exhib-ited throughout mankind and, most importantly, in the Body of Christ. We find another benefit of patience in James 1:2-4. "Consid-er it a great joy, my brothers, whenever you experience various tri-als, knowing that the testing of your faith produces endurance. But endurance must do its complete work, so that you may be mature and complete, lacking nothing."

When troubles come our way, the natural inclination is to rise up and fight it—usually on our own. But sometimes, God allows us to face tough situations for the purpose of building up our spiritual endurance and bringing about greater spiritual maturity. When we patiently rely on Him to get us through the valleys and the storms, He will bring another valuable blessing—peace.

In his letter to the church of Philippi, the Apostle Paul confirms that truth. "Don't worry about anything, but in everything, through prayer and petition with thanksgiving, let your requests be made known to God. And the peace of God, which surpasses every thought, will guard your hearts and minds in Christ Jesus."

That's the mindset that Kemper takes into each of his races and has relied upon for the duration of his professional career.

"I have that peace because I know that the triathlon doesn't ultimately define who I am as a person," Kemper says. "Whether I win a gold medal or not, I get my character as a person from my Lord and Savior Jesus Christ. I resound in that and hold true to that. That's who I am. That's who I'll always be and therefore I can never be let down. You can never be let down if your faith is in the Lord. I know that and I have peace with that and it gives me a lot of strength and patience going into my races."

The Extra Mile

1. Why do you think it's hard for most people to be patient?

2. What are some things that try your patience?

3. Do you find yourself to be more impatient with God and life circumstances, with yourself or with others? Why so?

4. Go back and read the scriptures from this chapter. Which of

them challenge you and your desire to be more patient? Which of them encourage you and give you hope that you can become more patient? Explain.

5. What are some things you can start to do today that will help you become more patient with God, with yourself and with others?

Find more of what the Bible says about patience by reading these passages: Lamentations 3:25, Romans 8:18-25, Galatians 5:22-23, Hebrews 6:13-15, 2 Peter 3:9 and James 5:7-8.

CHAPTER THREE

Live For God Not Men
Featuring Tamika Catchings, USA
Olympic Gold Medalist, Basketball

Ever since Tamika Catchings was a third grader playing on a boys basketball team, the WNBA All-Star and Olympic gold medalist has been learning valuable lessons about life.

Catchings learned about teamwork from her father and little league coach Harvey, who was also successful player in the NBA and Europe. She learned all about focus from Pat Summitt, her iconic head coach at the University of Tennessee. Catchings also learned about on-the-court leadership from college teammates Chamique Holdsclaw and Kellie Jolly Harper.

For the most part, these were enjoyable lessons and accompanied good times in her life. But one of the most important lessons she learned was a little more painful. During her senior season and just four months before the WNBA draft, Catchings suffered a devastating torn ACL. The injury forced the pro hoops hopeful to reevaluate her priorities and her values system.

"Basketball had become my god," Catchings says. "That's all I thought about. Sure, I went to school and made good grades, but at the end of the day, it was all about basketball. There was nothing more important to me."[1]

From an athletic standpoint, her plan was certainly working. As a high school player for Duncanville High School in Duncanville, Texas, Catchings made basketball history in 1997 by recording the only known quintuple double (25 points, 18 rebounds, 11 assists, 10 steals and 10 blocks). At Tennessee, she won a national championship as a freshman, was a four-time All-American, and was a shoe-in to be a first round WNBA draft pick. But her dream of playing at the highest level was now in jeopardy.

"When I got hurt, I feel like God was telling me to slow down and check my priorities," Catchings says. "He knew that basketball was important to me and He used basketball to get me to that point, but that wasn't all He wanted for me. He wanted our relationship to grow as well. So that injury opened my eyes to what I was missing. And since then our relationship has continued to grow."[2]

Catchings' newfound focus on God brought peace despite the uncertainty of her basketball future. That uncertainty didn't last long, though, when the Indiana Fever selected her with the third overall pick of the 2001 WNBA draft.

After sitting out that first season, she went on to become one of the game's most dominant players. Through the 2011 season, she had been selected to six WNBA All-Star games, four WNBA Defensive Player of the Year awards. That same year, she was also named one of the 15 greatest players in league history and won her first WNBA MVP award.

But for Catchings, her experiences as a member of the USA Basketball Women's National Team are hard to top. She played a key role in the U.S. team's overwhelming gold medal performances at the 2004 Athens Games and the 2008 Beijing Games. Catchings said the best part was representing her country and playing with the WNBA's elite.

"It is one of the most exciting things," she says. "Even when you talk about it, you can't fully describe the feeling. First and foremost, it's an honor to be considered one of the best in your nation. When you're there, everybody is watching you."[3]

Catchings often contrasts the highs of a WNBA and Olympic career with the lows of past injuries and childhood challenges. She understands now better than ever that the tough times were God's way of preparing her for the great times.

"All the things I've been through have given me a platform to be able to talk to people," Catchings says. "I grew up with a hearing problem and had to wear hearing aids. I grew up with a speech problem. I had glasses and braces. I dealt with all the things as a young child that you don't want to face. But it made me stronger and it helped me become the person that I am today."[4]

Now that Catchings understands her purpose—to use her platform to share God's love with others—she is better prepared to follow the principle the Apostle Paul taught the Colossian church. "And whatever you do, in word or in deed, do everything in the name of the Lord Jesus, giving thanks to God the Father through Him," he wrote in Colossians 3:17.

A few verses later, Paul reiterated that point with even more emphasis: "Whatever you do, do it enthusiastically, as something done for the Lord and not for men, knowing that you will receive the reward of an inheritance from the Lord—you serve the Lord Christ." (Colossians 3:23-24)

Catchings can attest to the fact that trying to please people always leaves us unfulfilled. God, on the other hand, will never disappoint. Even in her darkest moments, she always knew He would come through and meet all of her physical, emotional and spiritual needs. That's why Catchings, although very competitive, isn't consumed with winning or worried about her standing as a professional athlete.

"I could be mad sometimes about being one of the top players and not getting the publicity that maybe somebody else gets or not getting a deal like somebody else did," Catchings admits. "There are people like that. For me, whatever's mine, God will provide for me. Nobody can take that away from me."[5]

Whether that means a WNBA championship, more awards or another gold medal, Catchings knows that she has already won the ultimate prize: a relationship with God through the blood of Jesus and eternal life through His resurrection. And as Paul wrote in 2 Corinthians 5:15, "He died for all so that those who live should no longer live for themselves, but for the One who died for them and was raised."

"Even in competition, I don't want to lose myself in that," Catchings says. "I know that I'm competing for much higher purposes. I'm competing for God, not for other people or for myself."[6]

The Extra Mile

1. What are some of your gifts, talents and abilities? Do you spend most of your time using them for yourself, for your family, for the praise of others or for God's glory?

2. Can you think of a time when a circumstance slowed you down (i.e. an illness, a financial struggle, a family issue, etc.)? How have those kinds of challenges impacted your perspective on the purpose behind why you do what you do?

3. Go back and read Colossians 3:17, 23-24. What do you think it mean to do everything "enthusiastically" for the Lord?

4. What are some obstacles or attitudes that might be keeping you from giving God the glory in everything you do?

5. Make a list of some practical ways that you can start to use your gifts, talents and abilities for God's glory. What can you do today in order to see these things begin to show up in your life?

Find more of what the Bible says about living for God by reading these passages: John 15:8, Romans 12:1, 1 Corinthians 6:19-20 and Hebrews 13:15-16.

CHAPTER FOUR

Get Spiritually Fit
Featuring Lyndon Rush, Canada
Olympic Bronze Medalist, Bobsleigh

There's no such thing as an easy road to the Olympics. Athletes that reach the most elite level of competition go through a lengthy process that requires a costly sacrifice of time and hard work. To that end, the Olympian must have great discipline, unstoppable drive and a clear goal of achieving near perfect physical and mental fitness.

Canadian bobsledder Lyndon Rush knows all about the commitment it takes to become an Olympic athlete. He had previously learned about the disciplined life of an athlete while playing football at the University of Saskatchewan. But when he took a job working for his father while training for the 2010 Winter Olympics, Rush eventually realized that something had to give.

"I was doing bobsledding and real estate for my first four years," Rush says. "I decided I wasn't very good at either. I needed to go all out in one direction. So I decided I was going to quit working in real estate and just train year-round. My results got a lot better but my income went down. I wanted to do it the best that I could and not just do it halfway."[1]

As Rush was training for the Vancouver Games at the team facility in Calgary, the on-site chaplain, a man named Steve Sellers, talked to the bobsled driver about another kind of preparation that had nothing to do with his body or his mind, but rather something that would strengthen Rush's spirit.

"Leading up to the Olympics, (Steve) kept telling me, 'You need to be spiritually fit for the Games,'" Rush recalls. "Everybody knows you need to be physically fit, but he kept pounding that in me. I took that to heart and I really was (spiritually fit). I was in a really good place in my walk at that time."[2]

Rush wasn't a stranger to biblical principles. His Christian parents led the family in regular devotions and faithfully attended church. Rush even remembers the day he accepted Christ into his heart at the age of six. As he got older, some significant encounters with God at summer camp helped him recharge, but Rush can't remember a time in his life when didn't believe.

With his spiritual foundation solid as ever, Rush went to the 2010 Winter Olympics ready for anything. But there was no way he could know just how intensely his preparation would be tested. Rush was one of the favorites to win gold in the two-man race. After the first of four heats, he and his teammate Lascelles Brown were just one tenth of a second out of the top spot. That's when the unexpected happened. During the second heat, the Canadian duo crashed and Rush's medal hopes slid out of his reach.

"I was really devastated," Rush says. "I was really mad. I remember laying in the sled when it was still upside down and had finally come to a stop. But then my spiritual training kicked in and I said to myself, 'What do you have to be thankful for right now?' And immediately I thought about one of my teammates Chris Le Bihan who races with me in the four-man. His wife had a baby that same day. And I thought, 'Thank you God for that healthy little boy.'"[3]

Rush continued with that line of thinking as he slowly made his way to the finish line where the media awaited. Instead of saying "some stupid things," he was able to handle himself in a way that glorified God. Through his disappointing circumstance, Rush saw firsthand the fruits of his spiritual preparation and was able to put into motion what he had learned through Bible devotion and prayer.

"Happiness is about what's happening and sometimes you're not happy," Rush says. "But joy is a choice. You can develop joy. And the trick to developing joy is to think about what you have to be thankful for. No matter how bad things are, you can always think of something to be thankful for."[4]

That was the message Rush took to his four-man team as they prepared for their shot at Olympic glory. As they met to discuss the upcoming competition, he asked each teammate to share something for which they were thankful. The focus became less about winning and more about enjoying the moment and embracing the camaraderie that had developed over months of training. Rush's team was not considered a favorite to medal, but managed to turn some heads early on with runs that placed the Canadian crew in contention for second place. Not wanting to lose his laid-back, stress-free attitude, Rush began quoting Philippians 4:6-7 over and over again in his mind.

"Be anxious for nothing, but in everything by prayer and supplication with thanksgiving let your requests be made known to God. And the peace of God, which surpasses all comprehension, will guard your hearts and your minds through Christ Jesus." (NAS)

"As I said that over and over, the peace of God started to guard my heart and it took the weight off," Rush says. "My request was that I do my best and that my guys would be safe. I knew He would do that for me."[5]

With that prayerful attitude in his heart, Rush led his team to a bronze medal performance and missed winning the silver medal by just one-hundredth of a second. Days earlier, his spiritual fitness allowed him to glorify God in defeat. But on this day, Rush was able to give God the glory in an unexpected victory.

Rush's story really isn't much different from the situations we might find ourselves in each day. When things are going good, we experience varying levels of happiness. When things aren't going so well, we can feel depressed, anxious and disappointed. How we handle those circumstances, both the good and the bad, depends on our spiritual fitness.

Just like the Olympic athlete needs to be physically and mentally prepared, we as Christians need to be ready for whatever challenges may come our way. For the Olympian, it might require various methods of training that focus on athletic traits such as strength, agility, speed and endurance. But the successful life of a believer relies on spiritual characteristics such as the fruit of the Spirit found in Galatians 5:22-23: "love, joy, peace, patience, kindness, goodness, faith, gentleness, self-control."

In order to daily exhibit that kind of fruit, it requires routine participation in various exercises that are often referred to as the "spiritual disciplines." The Bible doesn't list these methods in one easy-to-find location, but we can find many of them prominently encouraged throughout scripture. Some commonly promoted disciplines include fasting, rest and solitude. But there are two spiritual training exercises that seem to be emphasized most: Bible devotion and prayer.

Athletes often have manuals that guide them through their

rigorous training. Christians have a manual too. It's called the Bible or God's Word. How else can we know what it means to follow Christ and be more like Him if we don't take time to read what God wants us to know?

David exhibited his understanding of this principle when he wrote such inspired exhortations as, "I have treasured Your word in my heart so that I may not sin against You" (Psalm 119:11) and "Your word is a lamp for my feet and a light on my path." (Psalm 119:105)

In a letter to his disciple Timothy written a thousand years later, the Apostle Paul echoed those powerful, but simple thoughts: "All Scripture is inspired by God and is profitable for teaching, for rebuking, for correcting, for training in righteousness, so that the man of God may be complete, equipped for every good work." (2 Timothy 3:16-17)

We are also reminded in Romans 15:4 that "whatever was written in the past was written for our instruction, so that we may have hope through endurance and through the encouragement from the Scriptures."

What those passages (along with so many others also found in the Bible) tell us is that reading God's Word is vital to our spiritual fitness. Like the Olympic athlete's proper training diet, the Bible feeds us truth for a solid foundation, direction for our life and advice on how to handle every situation we might encounter.

The other key element of a spiritually fit life is the consistent two-way communication with God most commonly referred to as "prayer." All elite athletes have a coach that gives them sound teaching and structured discipline in order to help them achieve their goals. But if that athlete never talks to the coach or fails to listen to the instruction given, success will be short-lived if ever attained in the first place.

For the Christian, that vital relationship is with God. It's a relationship that was made whole thanks to the death and resurrection of Jesus, "For through Him we both have access by one Spirit to the Father." (Ephesians 2:18)

Because of that access to God, we are able to take Him our worries, our fears, our hopes, our dreams and all of our needs. That truth is confirmed in 1 John 5:14-15: "Now this is the confidence we have before Him: Whenever we ask anything according to His will, He hears us. And if we know that He hears whatever we ask, we know that we have what we have asked Him for." This means that through spiritual disciplines such as Bible devotion, prayer and fasting, we can obtain answers to our questions, solutions to our problems, strength for our trials and wisdom for our most challenging decisions.

It's important, however, that you remember that these disciplines are *not* the key to salvation. We can only be saved when we accept Christ into our hearts and allow His blood to cleanse us of our sins. But once that relationship has been established, these spiritual disciplines can bring us closer to God and help us deal with the daily troubles this world brings.

That's exactly what Rush discovered during his Olympic journey. He had a relationship with God, but it was that spiritual fitness that came through consistent prayer and Bible devotion that allowed him to handle disappointment in a way that reflected Christ living in him.

"What's really important in life is what God wants us to do and how He wants us to be used and how we handle all sorts of situations, good or bad," Rush says. "You just have to give glory to Him. We don't really know what God's plan is for us. You need to remember that in good times and in bad times. For me, it was a bad time where God really used me. It was the worst thing that could ever happen in my mind. The way it all turned out, God was being glorified through the situation."[6]

The Extra Mile

1. What are some ways you try to stay physically fit? What are some of the areas that give you the most trouble? How difficult is it to stay disciplined in those areas?

2. What are some of the things you do to try to build up your spiritual fitness? Which ones do you find easy to do? Which ones do you find most difficult to do?

3. Can you describe the difference between those times you feel spiritually fit versus those times you feel spiritually weak?

4. Do you have a spiritual fitness plan? If so, what does it usually look like?

5. If you don't have a regular spiritual fitness plan, consider coming up with something that will allow you to daily participate in the spiritual disciplines of prayer and Bible devotion. Also consider other disciplines such as fasting, solitude and rest to help draw you closer to God and in turn bring you the strength and wisdom to be

more effective in your Christian walk.

Find more of what the Bible says about the spiritual disciplines by read-ing these passages: Matthew 6:1-18, Ephesians 3:14-19, Ephesians 6:18-20, 1 Thessalonians 5:16-18, 1 Timothy 4:5-6 and James 5:13-18.

CHAPTER FIVE

Put Up a Fight
Featuring Shannon Miller, USA
Olympic Gold Medalist, Gymnastics

Inside the heart of every Olympian is a "thirst for knowledge, an intense need for perfection" and "a relentless inner drive to succeed."[1] That might seem like a sweeping, grandiose statement, but maybe not so much when you consider the source.

Shannon Miller, the most decorated gymnast of all-time, spoke those descriptive words when asked what it takes to be an Olympian. Miller would know best. In two trips to the Summer Games, she won seven medals, including two gold. Some of her other international accomplishments include nine World Championship medals (five gold) and five Pan American Games medals (four gold).

There's another trait that Miller says can often be traced back to these super-charged athletes: a sort of sub-conscious approach to training that turns arduous work into pleasurable experiences.

"I'm not sure I even stopped to think about (what it took to become an Olympian)," Miller says. "I loved learning new skills. The medals were wonderful but they were always secondary to the skills. The hours got longer but I never felt that what I gave up was a sacrifice. I was doing what I loved and I was surrounded by the people that I loved. I also had a fairly normal home life with public school and living at home with my parents and siblings. As long as I had goals I was ready to move forward."[2]

Miller's hard work paid off in a big way. She qualified for her first World Championship at the age of 14 and won silver medals in the team competition and the uneven bars. Miller was cruising towards the 1992 Summer Olympics in Barcelona but ran into a major roadblock when she fell and dislocated her elbow while training for the upcoming World Championship in Paris.

"That injury was the turning point of my career," Miller says. "I had to decide. Was I going to give up or fight through that obstacle? I chose to fight."[3]

While much of her instinctive desire to push through the pain and disappointment was a product of naturally athletic DNA, Miller acknowledged that a deeply held faith, dating back to her childhood, ultimately provided the necessary strength and fortitude. And because of that faith, she was able to understand the answer to some even more difficult questions.

"When I wanted to ask, 'Why me? Why now?' I had to stop myself and just know that God had a plan for me," Miller says. "That injury ended up being the best thing to happen to my career. While I couldn't do certain skills until the arm healed, I was able to work other areas that I normally wouldn't have had as much time for. I became a stronger, more flexible, more well-rounded athlete than ever before."[4]

What seemed to be a potentially devastating circumstance turned out to be a proverbial blessing in disguise. Miller *was* a stronger, more flexible, more well-rounded athlete. And it showed at the 1992 Olympics in Barcelona, where she led the United States squad to a bronze medal in the team competition and captured four individual medals including silver in the all-around and the balance beam and bronze in the uneven bars and the floor exercise.

Miller used her debut Olympic experience as a springboard to international domination. At the 1993 World Championships in Birmingham, she took three individual gold medals, including the all-around contest. The next year in Brisbane, Australia, Miller repeated her gold medal performance in the all-around and added balance beam gold to the growing display of achievements.

Miller showed no signs of slowing down at the 1995 Pan-American Games in Mar del Plata, Argentina. She took home another four gold medals (team, all-around, uneven bars and floor exercise) plus a silver medal in the vault. Miller was on her way to becoming one of the greatest American gymnasts of all time.

Leading up to the 1996 Summer Olympics in Atlanta, Miller faced some new health challenges. She struggled with severe tendinitis in her left wrist and a pulled hamstring. Despite those issues, she won the U.S. National Championship and once again emerged as a gold medal favorite.

But this time, Miller was joined by one of the strongest groups of gymnasts to ever compete together at the Olympics. Miller, Dominique Dawes, Jaycie Phelps, Amy Chow, Kerri Strug, Dominique Moceanu and Amanda Borden became known as the Magnificent 7. The vaunted group proceeded to back up the moniker by winning team gold in front of the home crowd.

Miller also snagged her first individual Olympic gold medal with a winning performance on the balance beam. Even then, she fought through wrist pain with cortisone shots. Ultimately, she was unable to prevail in the all-around where she finished eighth.

But nothing she experienced at the Olympics, the World Championships or any other major competition compared to the battle she would face 15 years later. In early 2011, Miller was diagnosed with a rare germ cell tumor, a form of ovarian cancer. Confused and upset, the Olympic champion couldn't understand how this was happening.

"I had a 15-month-old little boy that needed me," Miller says. "Initially there was so much happening, so many tests, that I forgot to breathe."[5]

That's when Miller's natural tendency to fight through adversity kicked in. After an initial surgery to remove the tumor, she learned she would need nine weeks of chemotherapy.

"I was oddly at peace with the treatment," Miller says. "I knew it would be difficult, although I didn't realize how difficult until I got started. But I felt God's hand at work. I had to let go and trust that He had a wonderful plan for me and for my family. Cancer is never a good thing, but that experience has blessed me in ways I never would have imagined."[6]

As an athlete and more recently as a mother, wife and inspirational figure, Miller has come to understand the practical and spiritual applications of fighting through adversity. In particular, her understanding of God's Word has prepared her for unexpected difficulties that get in her way.

We shouldn't be terribly shocked either when we hit major bumps in the road from time to time. The Apostle Peter warned of this possibility when writing to the early Christians.

"Dear friends, don't be surprised when the fiery ordeal comes among you to test you as if something unusual were happening to you. Instead, rejoice as you share in the sufferings of the Messiah, so that you may also rejoice with great joy at the revelation of His glory." (1 Peter 4:12-13)

And like Miller found out, the bad things that are happening often serve a purpose down the road. The Apostle James encouraged the believers to, "Consider it a great joy, my brothers, whenever you experience various trials, knowing that the testing of your faith produces endurance. But endurance must do its complete work, so that you may be mature and complete, lacking nothing." (James 1:2-4)

James knew from experience that persecution, obstacles and problems would strengthen the Church and would help it follow through with the goal of evangelizing the world no matter what hardships might come its way.

This truth is also beautifully explained in Romans 8:28 where we are reminded that "all things work together for the good of those who love God; those who are called according to His purpose."

When Miller was hit with injuries, she was forced to work on other areas of training and put more effort into some of her underdeveloped skills. This gave her an edge that she previously didn't have in her competitive arsenal. And later on, the experience prepared her for a much more difficult battle against cancer.

For us, the fight might be against unemployment, disease, family discord or the loss of a loved one. But there will always be a purpose for the tough times. It might be about trusting God for finances, health and relationships. It might be about helping someone else work through personal loss. No matter what the trouble, there's no doubt that God has a plan in place to ensure that those things "work together for the good of those" who love Him.

And certainly there is no better example of tragedy working out for the greater good of God's plan than the torture, death and resurrection of Jesus. At the time, it seemed like the end of the world for His disciples and His family. But all the while, God knew exactly what was happening.

Jesus Himself struggled with the hardships He was going to face. While praying in the Garden of Gethsemane just hours before His death, Jesus was in such great anguish that, "He prayed more fervently, and His sweat became like drops of blood falling to the ground." (Luke 22:44)

In that prayer, Jesus asked God if another way to redeem mankind was possible, but ultimately went through the humiliating and painful death in order to fulfill His Father's plan of salvation.

"I have glorified You on the earth by completing the work You gave Me to do," he prayed before being betrayed and turned over to the Roman government. (John 17:4)

While our troubles might seem miniscule compared to what Jesus endured, they are still very real and can be very difficult to overcome. Thankfully, we're not in the fight alone. Miller understood that during her career and found that truth to be reinforced during her ordeal with cancer.

That's why she has always relied on a very simple scripture whenever any fear or doubt starts to creep in to her spirit: "For with God, nothing will be impossible." (Luke 1:37/Webster's Bible Translation)

"It doesn't matter what *my* plan is," Miller says. "It's *God's* plan that matters. There were many times in my career and in life that I had to remember to simply let go and let God. I hope that my story inspires people to never give up, never set limits on their potential and always rely on their faith as a source of strength."[7]

The Extra Mile

1. What are some obstacles that you have faced in life and how did you deal with those trying circumstances?

2. Can you describe the difference between trusting in yourself to get through tough times as opposed to trusting in and leaning on God?

3. Why do you think people often look for personal solutions to problems? What do you think ultimately causes people to turn towards God?

4. Do you believe that God has a purpose for your life? Explain.

5. How can understanding God's plan help you better fight through obstacles and adversity that comes your way?

6. How does Jesus' story change your perspective on things you might be dealing with today or in the future?

Find more of what the Bible says about fighting through adversity by reading these passages: John 17:1-4, Romans 12:12, 2 Corinthians 4:8-9, 2 Corinthians 1:3-4, 2 Timothy 4:7-8 and 1 Peter 5:10.

CHAPTER SIX

Discipline Your Self
Featuring Chris Byrd, USA
Olympic Silver Medalist, Boxing

When Chris Byrd arrived at the 1992 Summer Olympics in Barcelona, it would have been easy for the middleweight American boxer to get caught up in the hype, the pomp and circumstance, and the festive atmosphere that typically accompanies the most spectacular international sports event of modern history.

Four years earlier, Byrd narrowly missed the Games when he lost at the Trials to Todd Foster in the light welterweight classification. No one would have blamed the rising star for enjoying his accomplishment and taking in the Olympic experience for all of its worth.

Byrd did in fact enjoy Barcelona. He had a good time in the Olympic village and took full advantage of the special events planned for the elite athletes in attendance. But when the temptation to overindulge and put short-term desires ahead of long-term goals reared its ugly head, Byrd's self-discipline kicked in to high gear.

"I had a lot of fun meeting people and enjoying the activities, but my main thought was, 'performance,'" he says. "I went there to box and win a medal. So everything I did was done from the aspect of conserving my energy. I wanted to represent my country well."

Byrd's commitment to excellence paid off in the ring, where he roughed up four straight opponents en route to the gold medal bout. In the final, he lost a tough 12-7 decision against highly touted Cuban boxer Ariel Hernandez. But each time in the ring, the exuberant American fans in attendance energized him.

"It was so exciting to hear the chants of the crowd from the USA section," Byrd recalls. "It was the ultimate experience. You're in the Olympics. It makes you fight on. It makes you work harder. We had a nice crowd over there and they were going crazy. It was a great feeling to represent your country on the biggest stage in international sports."

Surprisingly, the unflappable boxer from Flint, Mich., was just a week away from his 22nd birthday when he made that fruitful trip to Barcelona. Or maybe it's not so startling considering that Byrd strapped on the gloves for the first time when he was five years old. His father coached him and both of his parents taught him the importance of self-discipline when most kids his age were still throwing tantrums when they didn't get their way.

But a year after Byrd won Olympic silver, something happened that drastically changed his outlook on life and the purpose behind those years of strict, disciplined training. Thanks to the influence of his wife Tracy, he accepted Christ after weeks of begrudgingly attending church before one of the pastor's messages finally hit home.

"When I got saved, the Lord just refocused me as far as my life goes," Byrd says. "I became very committed to my wife and my family. I wanted to be committed to the things that concerned Him."

Self-discipline was no longer just about training to win boxing matches and championship belts. Byrd was coming to understand the importance of an equally disciplined approach to his relationship with God and his most prized earthly relationships. While trying to balance his faith, his family and his career, prioritizing his life was a matter of survival.

"Because I trained so hard, I needed to be in the Word even harder so I wouldn't get trapped in all of the devil's snares," Byrd says. "When those arrows were coming my way, I needed to be in the Word so I could use that shield of faith. I had to wear my armor all the time."

Byrd's salvation experience and subsequent discipleship process had a profound effect on his boxing aspirations. After three professional fights in lower weight classes, Byrd felt inspired to move all the way up to the heavyweight division. At the time, he was a mere 175 pounds and the thought of even sparring against a bigger fighter sent chills down his spine. But there were no major players in his classification, so Byrd asked God to help him make the jump.

God answered his prayers in the form of a rapid weight gain. Within three months of his third pro bout, Byrd had eaten his way to a 193-pound frame that was at first mostly body fat mixed with a smattering of muscle. He eventually turned that extra weight into toned, well-defined volume while climbing the ranks and improving his career record to 26-0. Byrd suffered his first career loss against Ike Ibeabuchi in March of 1999, but he was too disciplined to let that setback keep him from pursuing excellence and a heavyweight belt. Just 13 months and four fights later, Byrd earned a last-minute shot at the World Boxing Organization (WBO) title against Ukrainian powerhouse Vitali Klitschko. Even though he had only seven days to prepare, he won the bout and the belt when Klitschko sustained an injury and withdrew after the ninth round.

Byrd lost that title six months later against Klitschko's younger brother Wladimir, but in December of 2002 claimed the International Boxing Federation (IBF) belt by defeating Evander Holyfield in a 12-round fight that resulted in an overwhelming unanimous decision.

By the time Byrd's career ended in March of 2009 with a light heavyweight technical knockout (TKO) victory against German boxer Mattias Sandow, he had fought in five different weight classifications, won two international heavyweight belts plus the United States Boxing Association (USBA) title, logged an impressive 41-5-1 professional record including 22 knockouts and racked up 275 victories as an amateur.

Byrd didn't accomplish these feats with raw natural ability although he did have plenty of that in his DNA. Rather, it was a disciplined work ethic and ability to avoid unnecessary distractions while staying focused on the important things in life that kept him on the path to success—even if at times that made him an uninteresting story to the general public and the mainstream media.

"I'm a very boring guy," Byrd jokingly admits. "When people interviewed me, the world of boxing wanted to have a least a little dirt. But I was too squeaky clean. It wasn't appealing to the world. I'm at home most of the time. When I was living in Michigan and wasn't training, I helped with the bus ministry at our church. Then I moved to Vegas and I trained at home and never really went anywhere besides church and to take my kids to school. But I had to stay on course for what I needed to do as an athlete and as a Christian."

Throughout his Bible studies, Byrd has learned the true purpose behind self-discipline. Much of his inspiration has come from a powerful sports analogy found in 1 Corinthians 9:25-27. In that passage, the Apostle Paul writes, "Now everyone who competes exercises self-control in everything. However, they do it to receive a crown that will fade away, but we a crown that will never fade away. Therefore I do not run like one who runs aimlessly or box like one beating the air. Instead, I discipline my body and bring it under strict control, so that after preaching to others, I myself will not be disqualified."

Pardon the pun, but Paul packs quite a punch in those four sentences. First of all, he makes the obvious point that competitors employ discipline (or self-control) by virtue of necessity (verse 25). But then Paul differentiates between earthly prizes (i.e. money, trophies, fame, acclaim, etc.) and Heavenly rewards (verse 26). Material possessions "will fade away," but God's ultimate "crown" is eternal life.

Next, Paul gives an example of what discipline looks like. He first advises believers not to run "aimlessly" or "box like one beating the air" (verse 27). In other words, have a plan of execution and know the purpose behind that plan. Byrd says that he looks at the 12-month calendar the same way he might approach a 12-round boxing match. And then at the end of each year, he reevaluates the game plan and makes sure he isn't falling into a comfortable state. Proverbs 21:5 backs up Byrd's assertion: "The plans of the diligent certainly lead to profit, but anyone who is reckless certainly becomes poor."

Another key to the disciplined life is accountability. Byrd is always quick to give credit for his success to those who helped him every step of the way, from his father who trained him to his wife who kept him on a proper eating schedule and, at her husband's insistence, quit her job as a flight attendant with American Airlines and traveled with him full time on the road as a protection from the boxing world's nefarious temptations. Again, Proverbs provides proof of this necessary companion to self-discipline. Proverbs 11:14 says, "Without guidance people fall, but with many counselors there is deliverance." Later on, Proverbs 27:17 reads, "Iron sharpens iron, and one man sharpens another."

"Discipline at the highest level of sports requires having people around you that truly care about you," Byrd says. "I had accountability with each and every person in my life. God surrounded me with a lot of good people, especially my wife. I've seen all of these athletes in the world losing their wives in divorce and because of extracurricular things. I wasn't going to go down that road, so I was very strict. I always had my wife with me."

And while the benefits of self-discipline are plentiful, we need to go back to 1 Corinthians 9:27 to find God's ultimate purpose behind the lifestyle choice. Like Byrd, the Apostle kept his body under "strict control, so that after preaching to others" he wouldn't "be disqualified." He knew that nonbelievers were watching his every move. He was well aware of the scrutiny that he was under and realized that all Christians would face that same level of judgment. Paul understood that the best way to protect his witness was to daily hold himself to God's standards.

Just because Byrd is now retired, that doesn't mean he can slack off on his disciplined ways. His example sets the tone for his wife and three children. And as a motivational speaker, he aspires to stay in shape and bring inspirational challenges to whoever his audience might be from one weekend to the next. Byrd is a walking picture of the truth found in Hebrews 12:11. "No discipline seems enjoyable at the time, but painful. Later on, however, it yields the fruit of peace and righteousness to those who have been trained by it."

In 2008, Byrd decided to embark on an even more disciplined life of Bible study and devotion. It wasn't easy at first, but as he saw those fruits come to bear, he continued to dive deeper and deeper.

"My prayer was, 'Lord, I want to know You more than I've known you in my whole Christian life. I want to be that close to You," Byrd explains. "How can I really be prepared for what the world's throwing at me if I don't know His Word? As a believer, that preparation and discipline comes first."

The Extra Mile

1. Why is self-discipline so important for an athlete? Why is it important for people in general?

2. In what areas of your life are you disciplined? In what areas do you struggle with self-discipline?

3. What are some examples of earthly "crowns" that you've won? How do those compare to the blessings from God and the hope of eternal life?

4. Why do you think self-discipline is so important when it comes to maintaining an effective Christian witness?

5. Do you have a plan that helps you stay disciplined? If not, what can you do today to start on a journey of self-discipline?

Find more of what the Bible says about self-discipline by reading these passages: Proverbs 13:4, Romans 6:1-13, Galatians 5:19-23, Titus 1:5-8 and Titus 2:11-14.

CHAPTER SEVEN

Be Faithful With Your Gifts
Featuring Ruth Riley, USA
Olympic Gold Medalist, Basketball

Ruth Riley is a member of a very exclusive club. Through the 2011 WNBA season, she was one of just six female basketball players to have won an NCAA championship, a WNBA title and an Olympic gold medal.[1]

Over the course of just five years, Riley led Notre Dame to its first NCAA Championship in 1999 (where she was named the Final Four Most Outstanding Player), was named Finals MVP award during the Detroit Shock's 2003 WNBA title run and earned a gold medal at the 2004 Olympic Games in Athens, Greece. It would be easy for Riley to boast about these accomplishments, but boasting isn't in her nature. In fact, the veteran pro athlete once claimed that she "was never the most talented athlete."[2]

Born in Kansas but raised in Indiana, the small-town farm girl grew up learning about hard work and commitment at home and her church. Riley took those lessons with her onto the basketball court where an adolescent growth spurt translated into significant success. At that point, there was no such thing as the WNBA. So beyond a possible college career, Riley's dream was to play on the world's biggest stage.

"Olympic athletes are mentally tough and very determined," Riley says. "They exhibit a high level of self-discipline, are coachable, and have an extremely strong work ethic. I've have always had the dream of playing in the Olympics and then from a young age I began to train with that ultimate goal in mind."[3]

Even though Riley was experiencing a high point in her professional career, there was no guarantee she would be named to the 2004 Olympic team. Instead, she had to be selected by a committee that would evaluate all of the talented athletes invited to tryouts and make decisions based on chemistry and roster balance. That's why Riley knew the key to her success would always be hard work and disciplined focus—the only two things she could control.

The 6-4 post player's attitude paid off when she was essentially the 12th and final athlete chosen for a team that included superstars like Sheryl Swoopes, Diana Taurasi, Tamika Catchings, Sue Bird and Dawn Staley. In fact, Riley found that her role was to prepare Lisa Leslie—arguably the best women's basketball player to play the game—by guarding her in practice. It was a difficult task and one that some less secure athletes may not have cared to tackle.

"It would have been very easy for me to just accept the fact that I was not going to play very much, and just go through the motions," Riley says. "But my faith calls me to work as hard as I can, and because of that, I was helping Lisa and the rest of our starters to prepare the best they could for the challenging games that they would face. I tried my best to exhibit humility and put the ultimate goal of helping my team win a goal medal ahead of any personal desires I might have had."[4]

For Riley, it was all about achieving a delicate balance of contentment in her role while maintaining a confident approach to her work that would not only prepare her teammates for their matchups but also make sure she was ready for any greater opportunities that might unexpectedly come along. It wasn't easy, but thanks to a measured dose of humility, Riley was able to fulfill her purpose on the team while achieving her childhood dream by winning Olympic gold.

"Without humility, my life would be a constant rollercoaster of excessive pride and devastating heartbreak," Riley says. "Whether it's frustration over my personal performance or heartache over relationships or experiences, I find that humility always leads me to a place where I can step back and see things from a different perspective. Humility leads me to a place of gratitude; a place where I am no longer fixated on myself and can better relate to others and better see a more positive solution."[5]

Riley has found that humility is the key to leading a faithful life of service to God and others. It has helped her be a trustworthy teammate on the court and away from the game. She has also been faithful in her approach to reaching out to the various communities she has impacted through basketball in addition to her work overseas in such places as Nigeria, Angola, Mali and South Africa. Health, education and ministry initiatives give Riley cause to put that faithful spirit into action.

Riley's Olympic story is reminiscent of a parable that Jesus told in Matthew 25:14-30. This story told of a man who went away on a long journey, but first gave his three slaves the responsibility of taking care of his material possessions. The man gave each slave a different amount of treasure (referred to as "talents") based on individual ability. When he returned, he discovered that two of the slaves had taken the talents and turned them into profit for their master. The third slave, however, took what he had been given responsibility over and hid it in a hole that he had dug out of the ground. Needless to say, the man was pleased to see what the two industrious slaves had accomplished and was equally displeased with the third slave's inability to overcome his fear of failure.

Jesus talked about the concept of faithfulness again in the Book of Luke, this time by explaining the parable's theme in terms that could be easily understood: "Whoever is faithful in very little is also faithful in much, and whoever is unrighteous in very little is also unrighteous in much." (Luke 16:10)

God has given every human being a certain measure of talent and ability. It might be natural athleticism or an outgoing personality. It might be a musical gift or an entrepreneurial sensibility. It could even be something as simple as a kind smile or a tender heart. And all God wants in return for these blessings is faithful service for His purpose—to glorify Him and to serve others.

Ruth Riley was born with a knack for sports and she eventually grew into a 6-5 frame that provided her the opportunity to gain notoriety as a professional basketball player. But it was her faithfulness to hard work and humility that truly allowed God to bless her with even more than she could have ever imagined. And now, she is truly thankful for what God has done in her life and continues to seek out even more chances to bless others with her gifts and their accompanying influence.

"After enjoying so much success in the sport that I love, I pray that people remember me for how I have been able to use that platform to make a positive difference in the world," Riley says. "Mostly, I hope that people see me living out my faith by how hard I compete and by treating others with the utmost respect and love."[6]

The Extra Mile

1. What are some things that come to mind when you hear the word "faithful?"

2. List some talents, abilities or gifts with which God has blessed you.

3. Can you relate to Ruth Riley's Olympic story? If so, did humility play a role in your experience?

4. Which of the two types of slaves can you best relate to, the two that took the talents and multiplied them or the one that fearfully buried his talent in the ground?

5. What are some ways that you can begin to use your talents, abilities and gifts to the fullest? What's stopping you from doing so? What can you do to remove those obstacles?

Find more of what the Bible says about faithfulness and using your God-given gifts by reading these passages: Matthew 25:14-30, Luke 16:1-13, Psalm 31:23-24 and Galatians 5:22-23.

CHAPTER EIGHT

Go Against the Grain
Featuring Jarome Iginla, Canada
Olympic Gold Medalist, Ice Hockey

Jarome Iginla is a Canadian ice hockey player. Left at that, his story is pretty much run-of-the-mill. After all, Canada is considered to be the birthplace of modern hockey and millions of young boys grow up hoping to play in the NHL. That was certainly the case for Iginla who was born in Edmonton, Alberta and fell in love with his country's national pastime at the age of seven.

But when you dig into Iginla's background, things get a lot more interesting, if not unusual. Take, for instance, his unique family history. His father Elvis Iginla moved to Canada from Nigeria to attend college. His mother Susan Schuchard moved to Canada from Oregon when she was 12 years old. The two eventually met and married. And although the marriage was short-lived, it did last long enough to produce a bi-racial son with loads of athletic talent.

Iginla has no memory of his parents being married. Most of his youth was spent with his mother and his grandparents although he did stay in regular, close contact with his father who is now a lawyer. "I don't know if it was normal," Iginla admits. "But it was normal to me."[1]

Iginla can't deny the compelling circumstances under which he was raised in light of his parents' very different religious beliefs. His father was a Christian who had grown up Muslim. His mother was Buddhist and put him through a Catholic school.

"(My mother has) always been Buddhist so that's a little

unique," Iginla says. "Growing up I didn't have a lot of other friends that had Buddhist parents. So that was different. There was (some confusion), but my mom was very good about it. She was very open. In that area I had a lot of questions because (Buddhists) do believe in different things. My mom was good at answering. She didn't force it on me by any means."[2]

Iginla says he has always believed in God but it wasn't something that truly became real to him until a fellow player at a hockey camp asked him a thought-provoking question. *What if there's no God?*[3]

It was a troubling question that eventually caused the 14-year-old Iginla to go to his father for spiritual advice. The very idea that God might not exist scared him. His father suggested that he ask God take that fear away. If Iginla felt peace, he would know that God, in fact, was real.

"That's probably my defining moment," Iginla says. "That was probably the most bothersome question that I can ever remember asking myself. When my dad told me that, it was probably the start of my own personal relationship. I'm at peace now."[4]

Perhaps it was Iginla's eclectic upbringing that helped him deal with the challenges of being bi-racial in a sport where only a handful of black athletes have excelled, although that number has steadily grown in recent years. But before Iginla's emergence as an NHL All-Star, it was that small group of pioneers that gave him ammunition against the naysayers.

"When I grew up, I was the only black kid on my team," Iginla says. "I was aware of that. I really was. I was very fortunate. My teammates were always great. But sometimes there'd be a small incident here or there with another team or with some parents in the crowd. Some kids would say, 'Why are you trying to be in the NHL? There are no black players in the NHL.' I remember those questions back then and honestly, it meant so much to me to be able to say, 'Oh yeah, there are black players in the NHL!' Grant Fuhr at the time was starring in Edmonton and winning Stanley Cups and he was an All-Star. I watched guys like Claude Vilgrain who played in New Jersey or Tony McKegney.[5]

"I am proud to be a black player in the NHL," Iginla adds. "I know how much those other guys meant to me so maybe there are kids that are having similar questions asked of them or maybe they're having some tough times. It would be an honor if I was at all a role model for kids that want to play in the NHL."[6]

Arguably, Iginla's diverse background developed his character and gave him a strong foundation for achieving great things. From that unique upbringing, he emerged as one of the greatest players in Calgary Flames history and has made multiple appearances in the World Cup, the World Championships and the Winter Olympics.

But perhaps none was more memorable than the 2002 Games in Salt Lake City, an event that Iginla describes as "one of the best experiences"[7] of his hockey career thanks in part to the opportunity to play alongside legends like Mario Lemieux, Steve Yzerman and Joe Sakic.

"I remember the first day showing up and seeing all those jerseys hanging and seeing mine over in the corner," Iginla recalls. "I was one of the younger guys and I had a makeshift area because there weren't enough lockers. But it was a huge thrill and I think I probably took a picture or something. It was difficult not to be in awe."[8]

And then the Canadians faced off against the host Americans in the gold medal game. It was a dream matchup for the sports broadcasters and fans alike. Not only did it feature some of the biggest NHL stars imaginable, there was also the sub-plot that found Canada seeking its first hockey gold in 50 years. From Iginla's perspective, the game absolutely lived up to the hype.

"It was probably the most exciting game I've been a part of," Iginla says. "It was so fast. The fans were so passionate. Half of them were American fans and the other half was Canadian. They were going at it the whole game. You get on the ice and go as hard as you can. You don't have time to be nervous. You get off the ice and you're nervous because you're watching as a fan. You want to win the gold medal so bad. It was every emotion—nervousness, excitement, adrenaline—all in one game."[9]

Canada went on to win that game, 5-2, and Iginla would claim another gold medal eight years later as part of the 2010 team in Vancouver. But all of Iginla's success likely would not have happened had he conformed to what was expected of him. Instead, his life was, and continues to be, all about going against the grain. In many ways, Iginla's approach to life lines up with the biblical principle of non-conformity. It's a concept that can be found throughout the Old Testament in stories about Abraham, Joshua, David and Daniel, to name a few, as well as the New Testament where Jesus and later on the Apostle Paul spoke often about doing things differently.

Paul wrote one of the most famous passages on the subject: "Do not be conformed to this age, but be transformed by the renewing of your mind, so that you may discern what is the good, pleasing, and perfect will of God." (Romans 12:2) In the New Living Translation, the first half of that verse reads, "Don't copy the behavior and customs of the this world, but let God transform you into a new person by changing the way you think." (NLT)

When Iginla was a teenage boy, he didn't have a full understanding of that scripture, but his actions proved him to be wiser than his years. Instead of conforming to the world—or in his case, listening to those who said he didn't belong on the hockey rink—Iginla pressed on and ultimately was able to achieve great things and give God glory in the process. Just like the person who follows after God's will, Iginla had to put up with some very negative comments that came his way. Jesus knew that non-believers would come against His disciples. So in John 17, He prayed to the Father on their behalf. He acknowledged in verse 14 that, "the world hated them because they are not of the world, as I am not of the world."

Jesus' statement will ring true for the modern day believer that stands out from the crowd. When we do things differently, those who haven't accepted His truth will try to tear us down with their words, tempt us to veer off course or in extreme cases resort to physical harm. And what might the "transformed" life look like today? It could be showing compassion for a social outcast. It could be forgiving the seemingly unforgivable. It could be sticking to God's plan for your life when that plan makes no sense to others and invites ridicule.

It might seem overly simplified, but there are some things you can do to live out Romans 12:2. First, stay rooted and grounded through a disciplined time of prayer and Bible devotion. If you know who God is and understand His heart, you'll be better equipped to discern between His voice and the voices of the enemy.

Secondly, avoid negative influences as much as possible. It

might be difficult to steer clear of everything that might try to point you in the wrong direction, but limit your time around people or even media influences that typically feed you a steady diet of conformist attitudes. Instead, find friends and media outlets that can uplift you and offer positive reinforcements in your quest to follow God's will.

And finally, in your regular prayer time and throughout the day, ask the Holy Spirit for the strength to make it through those difficult times when you are tempted to listen to ungodly voices or when you're thinking about giving up on your Christ-centered hopes and dreams.

Even now, when Iginla feels the pressure to conform to the world, he reminds himself of one simple truth that allows him to stay the course and continue to be a light in the world. "I feel a responsibility to God," he simply states. "I believe in Jesus. That's where my responsibility lies."[10]

The Extra Mile

1. Have you ever had someone tell you couldn't do something? If so, how did you respond?

2. Have you ever conformed to the world's expectations? If so, how did that impact God's calling on your life?

3. What are some ways that you have been tempted or pressured to conform to the world?

4. What are some things you've done to resist those temptations

and pressures?

5. Of the things listed that might help deal with conformity, which ones have you struggled to maintain? How would doing those things more consistently change your life?

Find more of what the Bible says about going against the grain by reading these passages: Romans 12, 1 Peter 1:13-16, John 15:18-25, John 17:6-19 and Proverbs 4:14.

CHAPTER NINE

Shine Your Light
Featuring Tobin Heath, USA
Olympic Gold Medalist, Soccer

In 2008, when most 20-year olds were still trying to figure out what they wanted to do with the rest of their lives, Tobin Heath was taking her first steps towards soccer stardom. Seemingly ahead of the curve for most of her career, Heath was the youngest member of the 2008 Olympic team (20 years, two months) while still making a big impact at the University of North Carolina, where she was a member of three NCAA National Championship teams.[1] But nothing stateside could prepare her for the sport's intense level of fan support around the globe.

"One of my favorite things about soccer is how the art and the passion of the game somehow unites people and nations and classes and races," Heath says. "Anytime you have an event like the Olympics or the World Cup, people get to enjoy it on such a huge scale."[2]

Between 2003 and 2006, Heath saw her first international action with stints on the U-16 (under 16) Women's National Team followed by significant time on the U-20 (under 20) squad. In 2007, she was part of the silver medal team at the 2007 Pan American Games in Brazil. Just five months shy of her 20th birthday, Heath made her first appearance with the senior national team at the Four Nations Tournament.[3]

Then, at the 2008 Olympics in Beijing, she got her first taste of gold medal glory. For Heath, the opportunity to represent one's country was undoubtedly the most special part of the experience.

"I don't think it's something you can put into words," she says. "I don't think it should be. The feeling that I was most shocked about was just seeing your country's flag being raised. I was shocked by how moved I was by that. I'm usually a pretty mellow person, but when that happened, I thought that was pretty cool."[4]

With many of the players from that Olympic team committed for two more years and some new young talent joining the fold, the U.S. squad was faced with extremely high expectations for the fast-approaching 2011 FIFA World Cup in Germany. After winning the 1999 World Cup, the program had suffered disappointing third place finishes in 2003 and 2007.[5]

In many pundits' eyes, this was the first real chance for the Americans to claim that elusive third World Cup title.

After three games in the group stage, Team USA did little to sway that opinion with dominant wins against North Korea (2-0) and Colombia (3-0). Even a 2-1 loss to the perennially talented Swedish team failed to plant any serious seeds of doubt.[6]

The competition predictably stiffened during the knockout stage, where the Americans were pushed by Brazil to a 2-2 quarterfinals finish before pulling away on penalty kicks (5-3). After a more typical 3-1 win against France in the semifinals, it seemed as if the United States team was destined for a return to the top spot on the podium.[7]

But what many onlookers didn't take into account was the inspired effort of a Japanese team that was playing with great emotion just three months removed from the devastating earthquake and tsunami in Tohoku.

In the World Cup final, the U.S. team seemed to have the upper hand after Abby Wambach's overtime goal at the 104-minute mark. But the Japanese stole back the momentum with a match-tying score at the 117-minute mark. Japan went on to secure its first World Cup title by outdueling the Americans 3-1 in a penalty shootout.[8]

The U.S. team was stunned and deeply disappointed. Heath felt many of those same emotions amid a crazy tournament that offered every competitive high and low imaginable. Yet her faith in God and trust in His purpose kept her from getting too caught up in either direction.

"During that time at the World Cup, it was a rollercoaster ride," Heath says. "But it was neat to just see God's hand on everything. It's more than just winning or losing. There are so many relationships that go deeper than that. He has a plan in it all. You have to trust that. Even though it's not the ideal outcome—I mean, everybody wants to be winners—you have to trust that God has a greater plan for this even when you can't see it.

"I can't even imagine going through life without my relationship with Jesus," she adds. "I need Him. I rely on Him. And not just in those crazy circumstances but in the day-to-day activities."[9]

Heath's strong faith was built on a solid foundation. She grew up in a Christian home that was "passionate about Jesus." But like many young people, Heath wanted to do her own thing for a while before realizing that she had a deep desire to personalize her belief in God.

"I stopped piggybacking off of my family's (faith) and wanted to figure out what it was all about," Heath says. "I got super interested in things and from there it's grown. Like anyone who has a relationship knows, the coolest thing about it is that it's infinite how much you can learn and begin to understand. That was something that grabbed me."[10]

Towards the end of high school and throughout college, Heath leaned on Christian friends and campus ministries to take the next step. And when she joined the senior national women's team, Heath found several teammates who shared the same spiritual goals.

"They're such an encouragement in my life," she says. "I have people praying for me and I'm praying for them. I can lean back on them. They strengthen me during those tough times. But even with my non-believing teammates, there is a great amount of unity and I truly believe that's God working. It's really cool in team sports when you're united around a belief or something you want to accomplish. Whenever you're working towards something greater than yourself, it's almost a selflessness that the Lord delights in when you're serving your teammate or your friend or your sister in Christ. That's why I love team sports."[11]

As Heath has excelled at the highest levels, her platform has continually increased. And despite her young age, she understands the importance of handling herself in a way that challenges, inspires and sends a message of hope to young girls, fans and anyone who might be watching from a distance.

Unlike some athletes, Heath wholly embraces the moniker of "role model" and the responsibility that accompanies it.

"I see it as a platform where you can pour love into others for Jesus," she says. "Becoming known or noticed in my sport isn't what drives me to work hard and want to be the best I can be. It's Jesus. That's why I play. I play to glorify Him. I worship Him with the gifts I've been given. Through that, I hope He can be glorified. That's my motivation when I step out on the field every day, whether it's at practice or during a game. I want to work as hard as I can in thankfulness for what He's given me. Hopefully some of that can come back to Him."[12]

But it's not always just about shining a light to the masses. Heath is also interested in impacting her teammates by setting an admirable Christian example and serving them with kindness and compassion. Some of her most opportune moments come when she is facing those aforementioned highs and lows.

"In the world of sports, you go through different ups and downs than what you might experience in normal life," Heath says. "You might be on top of the world playing or you might be sidelined with an injury. Your teammates see you through the good and the bad. They see where your foundation lies in those moments. You can also be there for them to share the love of Christ to them through those times when they're in need and desperate for some truth in their lives."[13]

Heath's desire to share the Gospel with fans, teammates and others within her circle of influence is perfectly aligned with the instruction Jesus gave His followers in Matthew 5:16. "Let your light shine before men, so that they may see your good works and give glory to your Father in Heaven."

Sometimes letting our light shine simply means living differently than those who aren't following Christ. One of the quickest ways we can stand out in today's world is to choose not to conform to its ways. It might be serving others instead of serving self or perhaps forgiving instead of holding on to bitterness and anger. It might be more overt like publicly thanking God for His blessings.

In Philippians 2:14, Paul gives more examples of how we can shine our light when he challenges the Church to, "Do everything without grumbling and arguing." Why? He explains in the next verse that living righteously before God will allow us to "be blameless and pure, children of God who are faultless in a crooked and perverted generation, among whom you shine like stars in the world."

In other words, when we strive to live like Jesus, we will shine His perfect light for everyone around us to see. Some might be drawn to that light and others might reject it. But ultimately, that's our charge—to let the love of God reside in our hearts and allow Him to open doors for us to share that love with others in an effort to bring them into a saving relationship with Christ.

Thankfully, there are no age requirements to be one of these shining stars. When Paul was mentoring a young disciple named Timothy, he made that very clear: "Let no one despise your youth; instead, you should be an example to the believers in speech, in conduct, in love, in faith, in purity." (1 Timothy 4:12)

Heath doesn't claim to be perfect. No one other than Jesus can make *that* claim. But that doesn't keep her from trying to live in a way that introduces as many people as possible to her Savior.

"My soccer career isn't about that worldly outcome in terms of winning or losing," Heath says. "It's about Him being known; not in a way that forces it upon other people but in a way that lets people know how He's transformed my life and how He's given me purpose and meaning and love and satisfaction. That's the message of Jesus. It's not a platform to impose on people. It's a platform to love people. Our God's going to be victorious. He's the Creator of the universe. I'm just a vessel to do my part with what I've been given."[14]

The Extra Mile

1. Tobin Heath has a large platform as a professional soccer player. Think of some other people that have sizeable platforms. What kind of influence do you those people have on others?

2. Who are the people in your circle of influence? How often do you think about the potential impact you might have on their lives?

3. What do you think it means to "let your light shine before men" as Jesus instructed in Matthew 5:16?

4. What are some things that are keeping you from shining your light today?

5. What are some ways that you begin to set an example for others that might exemplify God's love, compassion and righteousness?

Find more of what the Bible says about shining your light by reading these passages: Matthew 5:14-16, Matthew 28:19-20, 1 Corinthians 11:1, 2 Corinthians 5:20, Philippians 2:12-15, Philippians 3:17-18 and 1 Thessalonians 1:6.

CHAPTER TEN

Swim Upstream
Featuring Josh Davis, USA
Olympic Gold Medalist, Swimming

Whoever coined the phrase "different strokes for different folks" might as well have been talking about heralded US swimmer Josh Davis. It's not that the freestyler employed a radical method in the pool en route to three gold medals at the 1996 Atlanta Games and two silver medals at the 2000 Sydney Games. Rather, at the time of his highly successful career, Davis was quite a bit different in some other ways.

The first indication that Davis was swimming upstream, so to speak, came when he was about 13 years old. He wasn't very good in the pool; in fact, he was so bad that his first coach told Davis he should quit.

"He told me I should switch sports," Davis recalls. "But instead of switching sports, I switched coaches and everything was fine after that. It's amazing what happens when you get the right coach. We can all look back and see when a coach or a mentor or a teacher or a pastor or someone spoke into our lives and made a big difference. They believed in us. They encouraged us. And they taught us truth."[1]

Davis fell in love with the sport and worked so hard that by the end of his freshman year in high school, he was one of the best swimmers in Texas in his age group. He won his first state championship at the age of 15 and repeated the feat a year later. As a 17-

year old senior, Davis had gone from being so bad his coach thought he should quit to the fastest swimmer in the nation.

The San Antonio native received a full scholarship to the University of Texas, home of one of the top collegiate swimming programs. Davis admits he was "excited" for a chance at freedom.

"I could go to bed when I wanted. I could eat what I wanted. I could do, really, whatever I wanted to do. I was free," he says. "As long as I went to class and made swim practice, I was my own man."[2]

Davis says that early on at the ages of 17, 18 and 19 years old, he could get away with not always eating right and not getting quite enough sleep. But eventually, the party lifestyle he was enjoying along with many other teammates began to catch up with him. He started to struggle with school *and* with swimming. At the same time, Davis was beginning to feel a spiritual void in his heart. Through meaningful connections with campus ministries such as the Fellowship of Christian Athletes and Athletes in Action, Davis was challenged to take a hard look at his life.[3] That's when he uncovered some powerful truths about the physical body and its correlation to the soul. In 3 John 1:2, the writer says, "I pray that you may prosper in every way and be in good health physically just as you are spiritually."

And then in 1 Corinthians 6:19-20, Davis read these words: "Do you not know that your bodies are temples of the Holy Spirit, who is in you, whom you have received from God? You are not your own; you were bought at a price. Therefore honor God with your bodies." (NIV)

For Davis, his new goal was to first take care of three key

things—his mind, his body and his soul. "I'm a big believer that we need to develop ourselves and pursue excellence in all three areas to achieve balance and potential," he says. "To neglect one is to settle for less than your best."[4]

That meant some radical changes in his social life, his physical training and most importantly his spiritual commitment. He no longer viewed the campus as a massive dating pool. He no longer treated his body like a trash bin and stopped feeding it the wrong foods and drinking too much. And he no longer ignored his deepseeded need for a relationship with God through prayer and Bible devotion.

"I needed to memorize God's Word," Davis says. "I had to get it deep in my mind and my heart so that whatever situation I was facing, I would have the wisdom and power to make the best decision that would allow me to experience God's best for my life. It was huge when I began to memorize scriptures."[5]

Psalm 119:9-10 was the first verse he tackled. "How can a young man keep his way pure?" David writes. "By keeping Your word. I have sought You with all my heart; don't let me wander from Your commands." Just like in Hebrews 4:12, Davis began to experience the effects of the Bible as a "double-edged sword." The Word of God was now "real and relevant."[6]

But Davis' new lifestyle choices also brought a certain level of scrutiny and standoffishness from his friends. They were clearly not comfortable with the new creation in Christ that he had become. "When I committed my life to Jesus, the guys on the team thought I was nuts," Davis says. "They thought I had freaked out. I was part of the God squad, the Bible beaters, the Jesus freaks."[7]

Davis, however, had peace in his heart and knew that in

the long term, he would be much better off than those who continued to make poor decisions. It's a scenario he has seen play out
in many years of involvement at his alma mater.

"I've watched over 20 freshman classes come in," Davis
says. "These 18-year olds come to college and I watch them pick
their friends and I watch them date and I watch them break up and
it never fails. How they deal with their relationships ultimately
affects their performance in their sport. The negative decisions and
the negative consequences didn't have to happen."[8]

One of Davis' favorite Bible figures is the prophet Daniel,
an Israelite who had been taken along with several other young
men to live in his people's conquering nation of Babylon. When
Daniel stood up for his beliefs and refused to eat the king's food, he
did so at his own peril. He wasn't risking ridicule or embarrassment.
He was risking his very life. (Daniel 1:1-21)

And that wasn't the only time we find courageous acts of
integrity. When King Nebuchadnezzar built a gold statue in his likeness and decreed that everyone must bow down to it, Daniel's
friends Shadrach, Meshach and Abednego refused to comply. The
king ordered that they be tossed into a fiery furnace. Had God not
intervened and rescued them from the blaze, those three brave
young men would have paid the ultimate price for "swimming
upstream" and being radically different. (Daniel 3:1-30)

Daniel is also famously noted for his refusal to follow one
of King Darius' ill-advised laws that no man was allowed to pray to
anyone but the Babylonian ruler. Daniel maintained his routine of
praying three times a day and his enemies within the king's court
turned him in for his blatant disobedience. Darius was forced to
throw his beloved assistant into a den of lions, but again, the Lord
honored Daniel's faithfulness and kept him safe. (Daniel 6:1-28)

For Davis, swimming upstream meant living radically differently from his partying friends. It meant giving up some things that were deemed the norm for a college kid, but in exchange gaining better health, peace of mind and untold spiritual blessings. For Daniel and his friends, swimming upstream meant putting their lives in harm's way. For most of us reading this book, our experience will more likely resemble that of Davis, who gave up a few short-term pleasures for an immeasurable long-term payoff. There are some in this world who can better relate to Daniel. Having the courage to live for God and buck the societal norms is literally life-threatening in many countries such as North Korea, Iran, Saudi Arabia, Somalia, Iraq and Laos.[9]

In all cases, however, we can universally rely on God's Word for the strength to do what is right in His eyes. Deuteronomy 31:6 says, "Be strong and courageous; don't be terrified or afraid of them. For it is the LORD your God who goes with you; He will not leave you or forsake you." In 2 Timothy 1:7, we are also reminded by the Apostle Paul that fear does not come from God, but is rather a by-product of the enemy's evil and twisted plans to destroy those who might stand against sin and injustice.

For Davis, the choice was an easy one to make. He has reaped the benefits of living by 1 Peter 1:14-15, which advises believers not to be "conformed to the desires of your former ignorance. But as the One who called you is holy, you also are to be holy in all your conduct."

But Davis wasn't compelled to strive for holiness because he felt forced to do so. Neither did he start allowing the Holy Spirit to gently nudge him towards a more Christ-like walk in order to selfishly obtain His blessings or because of a misguided belief that a holy lifestyle would help him win. Davis says the most important spiritual principle he ever learned throughout the process was that his relationship with Christ wasn't based on what he had to do to please God, but what God was pleased to do in him, through him and for him. As he read the Bible, the message of God's incomprehensible unconditional love startled Davis. It was so different from the world of sport where everything depended on today's performance.

Yes, success was sweet, but the minute he wasn't a winner it turned sour and all of the perks that came from winning were literally gone overnight. As he began to understand that Christ died to give him a worth that would never go away, that unconditional love softened his hard, pleasure-seeking, self-centered heart. The affirmation he had been looking for in the all the wrong places suddenly grabbed him and would not let him go.

"The funny thing about love is that you find it changes you," Davis adds. "You want to look good and wear those nice clothes so that your boyfriend or your girlfriend isn't embarrassed with you. How much more should you want to live differently for the Lord because you want to show gratitude for Him? He's your number one fan and He'll never leave you."[10]

Motivated by his deep gratitude for the love, mercy and grace that God had bestowed upon him, Davis desired then and continues to desire now to please God and to give Him glory by reflecting His character no matter the outcome of any given race or circumstance in his life.

"God doesn't need me to win," Davis says. "He shares the glory with no man. But He gets the greatest glory when we reflect His character in the wins and especially the losses. Truth is, I can't do anything apart from His love and grace and He can't love me anymore than when He died on the cross for me. His never failing love is the only lasting motivation for a healthy Christian life. And win or lose, burn in flames or not, I trust in Him."[11]

The Extra Mile

1. What does it look like to "swim upstream" in your world?

2. Why is it so difficult to live radically different than the mainstream of modern society?

3. Read the three stories in Daniel. Put yourself in the shoes of Daniel and his friends. How would you have responded to those challenging circumstances?

4. What are some areas in your life where you find it especially different to "swim upstream" and deny yourself of "the desires of your former ignorance" as it says in 1 Peter 1:14?

5. What are some ways that you can start today in an effort to live out the exhortation of 1 Peter 1:15 (be holy in all your conduct)?

Find more of what the Bible says about the courage to swim upstream by reading these passages: Daniel 1:1-21, Daniel 3:1-30, Daniel 6:1-28, Matthew 10:28, Romans 12:12 and 2 Timothy 1:7.

CHAPTER ELEVEN

Give Credit Where Credit is Due
Featuring Chad Hedrick, USA
Olympic Gold Medalist, Speed Skating

For a long time, Chad Hedrick made some fair assumptions about his success. His father owned and operated a roller skating rink in the Houston suburb of Spring, Texas, where he began skating as a two-year old. Hedrick also developed his natural ability with a great deal of hard work and eventually progressed into an elite athlete. And that's why, in his mind at least, he became one of the most decorated American speed skaters in Olympic history and a revolutionary figure within the inline speed skating community.

But after the 2006 Games in Torino, Hedrick had an epiphany about the true source of his good fortune.

"With all the success I've had, I never really acknowledged the Lord," Hedrick admits. "I never appreciated what He's given me to work with and the life that I have and the people around me and the situations I had growing up."[1]

Up until then, Hedrick's status as a lone ranger created an imaginary "me against the world" reality that followed him into the 2006 Olympics.[2]

"I had the attitude that the world was after me," Hedrick says. "It was me on the ice trying to show everybody that I was the best in the world. I was this major, fierce competitor that hated to lose. I had this tough personality because of my competitive drive. I was really harsh and trying to display this strong shell to my competitors."[3]

Some might find it hard to argue against the positive results Hedrick yielded with that mindset. Before switching to the ice, he was a dominant inline skater with 93 national championships and 50 world titles. Hedrick also set a combined 12 U.S. and world roller and inline skating records.

After watching the 2002 Olympics, Hedrick was inspired to try ice speed skating. Just 18 months later, he broke the all-around combined points world record in Hamar, Norway, and went on to break five more world records leading up to the 2006 Olympics. In Turino, Hedrick won gold in the 5,000-meter race and added silver in the 10,000-meter race and bronze in the 1,500-meter race.

Away from the ice, Hedrick was living a fast and furious lifestyle that had little to do with the Christian faith that he loosely claimed. As far as he was concerned, all that was required to be a Christian was to simply believe in God. Before long, he had earned the moniker "Bad Chad," thanks to a reputation as a party boy, a less than gracious opponent and critical teammate.

That all changed when he met his wife Lynsey whom Hedrick married in June of 2008. Through her influence and the example set by her family, he quickly learned that there was much more to the superficial Christian life he had been living, and that a deeper relationship with God was available to him. Hedrick was a changed man. And by the time the 2010 Olympics in Vancouver came, people had taken notice.

"The skating fans realized the difference," Hedrick says. "The other skaters were telling me every day that I looked like I was having so much more fun than I used to. My whole outlook on life was completely different. I used to want to throw my skates when I lost but then I realized that whatever I do on the ice, whatever place I finish, there's a whole purpose to the day. There was a lesson to be learned no matter if I won or lost. God was molding me and shaping my personality."[4]

There's a stark difference in the lives of individuals that take credit for personal success and those that make a concerted effort to give God the glory for the good things that come their way. In Judges chapters 13 through 16, we find a perfect example of this principle as exhibited in the life of Samson.

Samson was one of Israel's judges—appointed rulers that predated the kings and oftentimes served as military leaders to guide the nation through tumultuous times. Samson is often referred to as the strongest man in the world. His strength came from a covenant his parents made with God. Samson would maintain his power as long as a razor never touched his head. Samson was also notorious for his greatest weakness—beautiful women. It was, in fact, a Philistine woman who tricked Samson into revealing his secret so that the enemy could defeat him. But his bigger problem was pride that allowed the mighty man's ego to swell out of control. It was Samson's refusal to acknowledge God's providential presence in his life that ultimately led to his demise. Perhaps Samson could have benefited from some advice that would be given by one of Israel's future kings. In Proverbs 16:18, Solomon (often referred to as the wisest man in the world) wrote, "Pride comes before destruction, and an arrogant spirit before a fall."

Count on it. Every time you start to feel like you're on top of the world and you can do no wrong, you turn the corner and smack your face right into a proverbial wall that wasn't supposed to be there. An equally painful (if not downright embarrassing) tumble is typically the second half of such a scenario. It might not be as ugly as what went down with Samson who lost his strength, had his eyes poked out and was committed to a life of slavery.

But the result of out-of-control pride and a refusal to acknowledge God's hand in our lives can still result in some fairly unattractive consequences. On the other hand, the Bible tells us about a better way to live. In 1 Corinthians 10:31, the Apostle Paul wrote, "Therefore, whether you eat or drink, or whatever you do, do everything for God's glory."

It's interesting that Paul used the word "everything" in that passage. There's not much wiggle room when all-encompassing words are in play. That's because Paul took Jesus' command for His followers to "give glory to your Father in heaven" quite literally. When you have food to eat, give glory to God. When you have something to drink, give glory to God. When you get a paycheck each week, give glory to God. When you get out of bed in the morning, give glory to God. When you run in a race, compete in a competition or play in a game, win or lose, give glory to God.

By the time Samson realized this truth, he was already the punch line of a bad Philistine joke. Yet when he had the chance to avenge his betrayal, God was faithful to give him his strength back for one last mighty act of greatness (read Judges 16:21-31).

Thankfully for Hedrick, he avoided the nasty, life-altering fall that ultimately took Samson out of the game. He learned to turn his personal victories into opportunities to allow God to shine through him. Hedrick didn't win a gold medal at the 2010 Olympics in Vancouver but he did bring home a silver medal in the Team Pursuit and a bronze medal in the 1,000-meter race. Despite what some might have seen as a disappointing result, Hedrick said he now has something much more important—a reprioritized life that places God first, family second and the quest to make a name for himself way down the list.

"God gave me something special," he says. "I want to show the world and bring glory to His name with the talent that He gave me."[5]

The Extra Mile

1. What is one of your major accomplishments in life?

2. Was the accomplishment a result of your hard work, your natural abilities or something else?

3. Were you tempted to take the credit for that accomplishment?

4. Have you ever experienced the principle found in Proverbs 16:18? If so, explain.

5. On the other hand, what have you seen take place when you've given God glory for the good things that have happened in your life?

6. What are some ways that you can begin to give God more glory through your life?

Find more of what the Bible says about giving God the glory by reading these passages: Philippians 1:9-11, Galatians 6:14, 1 Peter 2:12, Romans 1:18-21, Psalm 115:1, 1 Corinthians 1:27-31

CHAPTER TWELVE

Play With Passion
Featuring DeLisha Milton-Jones, USA
Olympic Gold Medalist, Basketball

For many athletes, there are some age-old questions that ponder the appropriate level of competitive zeal: When does aggressive play become *too* aggressive? Can you play with *too* much intensity? Is there a line that can be crossed? And if so, where exactly *is* that line?

DeLisha Milton-Jones is among those who have struggled to find that balance. Whether starring at the University of Florida, leading the Los Angeles Sparks to a pair of WNBA titles (2001 and 2002) or playing a key role on two Olympic gold medalist teams (2000 and 2008), she has always tried to give her best and play with high levels of passion. For Milton-Jones, that means making full use of her unique physical attributes—namely, an 84-inch wingspan that might typically be seen on a seven-foot frame and not on the body of a 6-1 woman.

"I have been known for my wingspan since day one and I even make some jokes about myself to other people about it," Milton-Jones says. "I say that when my mom gave birth to me, they pulled me out by my arms instead of with the forceps. That's how my arms got stretched out of proportion."[1]

It's easy these days for Milton-Jones to have fun at her own expense. After all, those arms have helped make her one of the best defensive players in the WNBA.

"I definitely use (my wingspan) on the defensive end more

than I do offensively," she explains. "I keep them coiled up so I look like the normal, average player out there. When people get comfortable and put the ball in front of me, the forget that my wingspan is as long as it is and before they know it I've taken the ball out of their hands and we're going the other way."[2]

Milton-Jones didn't always get joy from a playing style that was naturally aggressive and intense. In fact, for several years she struggled with that aforementioned balance between athletic excellence and her Christian witness. In an effort to make sense of things, she often went to her husband Roland Jones, a former collegiate and European professional, for advice. She also had some in-depth conversations with WNBA legend and former teammate Lisa Leslie. Milton-Jones even went to her mother Beverly Milton for counsel on the matter.

"If I'm not being competitive then I just feel like I'm getting punked while I'm out there on the court," Milton-Jones says. "How do you get to the point where you're competitive but you don't lose your godliness? It really did bother me that people would view me as a dirty player when I'm just highly competitive. I'm going to use every inch or every margin that I can within the rules of the game to my advantage. Some people look at me and think I'm doing too much. But I'm just willing to do whatever it takes to win."[3]

Milton-Jones has also confided in Sparks team chaplain Camille Wooden who has always appreciated the athlete's caring nature and infectious smile. According to Wooden, Milton-Jones is known as "Sunshine" away from the game, but on the court, her ferocious play has garnered the nickname "D-Nasty."

"I've had conversations with (DeLisha) and some other players about how to let your light shine on the court," Wooden says. "There's that tension between trying to be aggressive while still trying to remain holy. You can let it get the best of you sometimes on the court. That's just like life period."[4]

It took a few years before Milton-Jones figured that out, but now, she's able to enjoy the game more than ever and play with equal amounts of passion and biblical integrity.

"You can go out there and push and fight and shove with the best of them," she says. "But you can't let anyone get you to the point where it makes you think ungodly things or say ungodly things or do ungodly actions. Once I was able to put a harness on (my intensity) and control it, a change came about."[5]

Milton-Jones' story is fairly common among Christian athletes, especially those that compete at an elite level. But they can all take heart in knowing that God desires for them to give their best and play with maximum effort. He wants the same thing for every one of us no matter what position, title, job or responsibility we might hold. Verification for this truth can be found in Romans 12:11: "Never be lacking in zeal, but keep your spiritual fervor, serving the Lord." (NIV)

The Apostle Paul also wrote about this subject in a letter to the Christians of Corinth: "Be steadfast, immovable, always excelling in the Lord's work, knowing that your labor in the Lord is not in vain." (1 Corinthians 15:58) In other words, whether it's in our work, our play or anything we do, it should be approached with a passionate heart and a strong desire to exhibit excellence with the intentions of bringing glory to God. But we can't play with true godly passion until we have a relationship with the One who gave us our talents and abilities in the first place. Only then can we live out the greatest commandment that Jesus talked about in Matthew

22:37. "Love the Lord your God with all your heart, with all your soul, and with all your mind."

Milton-Jones learned to embrace that spiritual charge at a young age. When she was 11 years old, she nearly drowned in her town's recreational pool one summer. From that experience, she was able to be thankful for life and never take it for granted. It also fueled her passion to use the platform as an international women's basketball star to encourage young girls to likewise pursue their God-given dreams with passion.

"It's okay to be a radical for Christ," Milton-Jones says. "It's okay to stand up and be heard and not be shy about being a Christian. You don't have to be boastful or get in people's faces but it's about being confident and knowing that at the end of the day, no matter what happens, you're taken care of. You're covered."[6]

The Extra Mile

1. What is something that you're passionate about?

2. Do you think it's possible to have too much passion or become too aggressive in your outward expressions?

3. Do you believe that Christians have a responsibility to be excellent in everything they do whether that's reflected in their work, responsibilities, recreation, etc.?

4. Go back and read Matthew 22:37. How do you think a full embrace of that scripture might change the way you view your passionate pursuits and your desire for personal excellence?

5. What are some things you can start doing today that will unlock your access to godly passion and set you on a path of excellence in everything you do?

Find more of what the Bible says about living life with passion by reading these passages: 1 Corinthians 9:24-27, 1 Corinthians 10:31-33, Philippians 3:12-14 and 2 Timothy 2:15

CHAPTER THIRTEEN

Serve It Up
Featuring Michael Chang, USA
Olympic Athlete, Tennis

Many elite professional athletes often follow a natural progression. They get famous, make lots of money, set up a foundation, and when they retire, put even more time and resource into that charitable effort.

It's impossible (not to mention unadvisable) to judge the intent of anyone who follows that path. Still, there's a good chance that many of them get involved in the giving game for one of the following three reasons: it's expected of them, it makes them look good or it provides a renewed sense of purpose.

But for Michael Chang, the passion to serve was born out of something deeper—a heartfelt desire to use his prestige as a tennis champion in a sincere effort to be the hands and feet of Jesus.

Chang has come to understand the truth found in Philippians 2:13: "For it is God who is working in you, enabling you both to desire and to work out His good purpose."

By his own admission, there's really no other way that Chang can explain such an unlikely story. His father Joe was born in China and came to the United States for graduate school. His mother Betty was the daughter of a Chinese diplomat who, during the intense civil unrest of the 1940s, escaped to America with his family.

Chang's parents eventually met, fell in love and married. Somewhere along the way, they innocently passed along a love of tennis to both of their sons. Chang picked up the game at the age of seven, but not like many of his peers (i.e. Jim Courier, Andre Agassi, etc.) who were sent to high profile tennis academies in Florida.

"I would play on weekends and then I started playing in some junior tournaments," Chang recalls. "Before we knew it, I was playing in national tournaments and that just took it to a whole new level. I'd never thought about turning professional or anything like that. If anything, my mom and dad were thinking that maybe it would be nice for (my brother) Carl and I to get a college scholarship or something."[1]

When Chang turned pro at the age of 16, his career became a family affair. After a brief pro career of his own, Carl Chang became his younger brother's coach. And his mother Betty was a fixture on the tour from day one.

"My mom quit her job and followed me for the first four years of my career," Chang says. "That was not only a sacrifice on her part. It was a sacrifice on my dad's part as well."[2]

Her act of service paved the way to early success for Chang who just a year into his professional journey found himself contending for the 1989 French Open. On June 5, Chang took the court against legendary three-time French Open champion Ivan Lendl. It was an emotional time for Chang, who had been watching the events of the Tiananmen Square Massacre unfolding since a day earlier.[3]

After dropping the first two sets (6-4, 6-4) and going down a break on the opening of the third set, Chang fought back to win 6-3 and force a fourth set. In that frame, he began suffering from severe cramps. Even with a 2-1 lead, Chang seriously considered retiring from the match.

As he walked towards the chair umpire, Chang got no further than the service line before he felt the Holy Spirit convict him.

Michael, what are you doing?

Even though it made perfect sense for Chang to quit, he continued to hear the Spirit encouraging him to keep playing, reminding him that the results weren't for him to worry about but that instead his job was to "go out there and compete and give 100 percent."[4]

"God calls us to go out and work hard and to give our best and for us to go through life finishing the race and not quitting along the way," Chang says. "That's very true for the Christian life but for me on that day, my race to finish was that particular match. So I said, 'Alright Lord. I'll try to finish this match.' My primary goal was then finishing the match and not to worry about winning and losing and to trust Him for all of that. But I still knew I probably wasn't going to win."[5]

Chang turned around and went back to his position on the court. He played the next point and the next point and the point after that. If he had an opportunity to hit a winner, he would go for it. Then suddenly, Chang started winning points, those points turned into games, and before he knew it, he had fought back to win one of the most compelling five-set matches in the history of Grand Slam tennis.

"I go back sometimes and I look at that video tape and even after I'm done looking at it, I still can't understand or comprehend how that match was won," he says.[6]

Even then, Chang understood that his victory—which ultimately led to a historic French Open championship—had little to do with the elevation of his career, but was instead an opportunity for God to increase his platform and in that specific moment for the purpose of lifting the spirits of the Chinese people.

"The match with Lendl is evidence of what God can do and (evidence of) His power," Chang says. "Certainly, being 17 years old, I was not expected to win and I wasn't expected to come back from two sets down and to do it against Lendl. But God has His funny ways of showing His power and He has His funny ways of allowing the weak things of the world to shame the strong and allowing the ordinary things of the world to become extraordinary."[7]

It's hard to know for sure, but there's a logical line of thinking that says Chang might not have achieved the same celebrity status on the tour had he not won that match and the French Open. But because of the epic victory that captivated tennis fans worldwide, Chang was arguably blessed with more open doors and a much larger platform from which he could share his faith in Christ.

In 1 Peter 4:10-11, the Apostle wrote this telling letter to the early Christians: "Based on the gift each one has received, use it to serve others, as good managers of the varied grace of God…if anyone serves, it should be from the strength God provides, so that God may be glorified through Jesus Christ in everything."

Chang, who later went on to compete in the 1992 and 2000 Summer Olympics, has done his best to abide by this Christ-centered principle. He has been blessed with an amazing gift and has used it to serve others. And because Chang overcame such incredible circumstances as an undersized Chinese teenager dealing with adverse physical conditions, he was later able to serve from a position of reliance upon God's grace.

That led to the creation of the Chang Family Foundation

in 1999, established to "introduce the Good News of Jesus Christ to the world through local community and international programs."[8]

Chang also spearheaded the creation of the Christian Sports League in 2002 with the purpose of providing a "vehicle for local churches and organizations" in Seattle and Orange County "to share the Gospel through organized and competitive sports."[9]

All of these endeavors are the byproduct of Chang's desire to impact people's lives for the sake of sharing God's love. He takes his cue from the example set by Jesus during His time on earth.

"The Lord set such an incredible example for us," Chang says. "Here you've got the Son of God. He brings 12 disciples under his wing. It's amazing the patience that He shows them and the love that He shows for all the people He comes into contact with, whether that's to heal them or fellowship with them or to embrace them. That was especially true for those who were rejected. You're talking about tax collectors who were hated by the people. You're talking about the prostitutes who didn't get any respect. You're talking about the lowly fishermen. Jesus wasn't calling the high priests and the Pharisees to be His disciples. He was calling regular, ordinary people."[10]

According to Chang, the countercultural nature of Christ's approach is "mind boggling"[11] and scripture tells us that His heart of service made the religious leaders question His claim to be the Son of God. Yet in His own words, Jesus told His disciples that He "did not come to be served, but to serve, and to give His life—a ransom for many." (Mark 10:45)

We gain an even greater understanding of Christ's example as the ultimate servant in Philippians 2:5-8. In that passage, the Apostle Paul explains that, "He emptied Himself by assuming the form of a slave, taking on the likeness of men," and "humbled Himself by becoming obedient to the point of death—even to death on a cross."

You can't get much more countercultural than that. At the time, Jesus was one the most polarizing public figures, yet He was extremely popular because of His revolutionary teachings, His unusual compassion for the dregs of society, and of course His incredible miracles.

Since the time of Christ, mankind has unfortunately seen far fewer servant leaders than the stereotypical self-absorbed variety. The condition that often strikes those in authority is nothing more than a simple case of pride. It's a problem we all have no matter what position we may or may not hold. Whether rich, middle class or poor, people have a natural inclination towards caring about themselves more than others.

Jesus gave a sharp warning to those who are guided by this mindset in John 12:25: "The one who loves his life will lose it, and the one who hates his life in this world will keep it for eternal life."

And sometimes people shy away from serving because it's uncomfortable, difficult and messy. But for the Christian, the opportunity to share the Gospel message is so often sparked by a random act of kindness towards someone in need. Chang calls service "one of our greatest witnessing tools."

In 1 Corinthians 9:19, Paul used a historically meaningful analogy when describing how the selfless act of serving can change lives: "Although I am a free man and not anyone's slave, I have made myself a slave to everyone, in order to win more people."

Thankfully, serving others doesn't require a submission to slavery (as Paul wrote in an effort to make a powerful point). But there is a heavy responsibility that the believer is challenged to accept whenever they choose to take up the cross as Jesus described in Luke 9:23.

"God has given us a platform to proclaim His name," Chang says. "Quite honestly, God is God. He doesn't need me to do His work. But He uses me because I want to be used by God. It's an honor and a privilege to be able to be a part of His plan."12

The Extra Mile

1. Michael Chang talks about how his family impacted his desire to serve others. Can you point to any circumstances in your life that have inspired you to serve?

2. What are some gifts that you feel like you can use to serve others? Have you had the opportunity to use those gifts? If yes, how? If no, what has kept you from doing so?

3. What aspects of Jesus' life are the most inspiring when it comes to the act of serving?

4. What are some ways that serving can be uncomfortable, scary or messy? Have those things ever kept you from reaching out to someone?

5. What are some things you can start doing right away to put your gifts into action as a means by which you might impact someone's life?

Find more of what the Bible says about serving others by reading these passages: Proverbs 19:17, Matthew 5:16Matthew 22:36-40, Matthew 25:31-40, Mark 9:33-37, Mark 10:42-45, Luke 6:38, John 13:4-5, Acts 20:35, Romans 12:10-11, Philippians 2:3-13, James 2:14-17.

CHAPTER FOURTEEN

Take the Narrow Road
Featuring Bobby Jones, USA
Olympic Silver Medalist, Basketball

Bobby Jones is notoriously honest. We're not talking run-of-the-mill honesty here, the kind that purports to tell the truth most of the time but sees fit to occasionally hedge a little bit for the sake of saving face, avoiding embarrassment or getting ahead in life.

No, Jones is closer to the neighborhood of George Washington honesty, where integrity trumps self-preservation, dignity and personal gain.

During his stint with the Philadelphia 76ers, Jones recalls two incidents that best illustrate just how radically honest he was in comparison to the average player. In a game at San Antonio, the ball was going out of bounds and Jones tried to save it. He had inadvertently blocked the official's view in the process. After retrieving the ball from the stands, the official discreetly asked Jones if he'd touched the ball. At that moment, Jones had a funny thought.

I get to play and I get to ref too.

To those who knew him best, Jones was instinctively honest with the official in his response. "No, I didn't touch it," he said.

"Red ball!" the satisfied referee shouted.[1]

That particular situation worked out in Jones's favor, but that wasn't the case about two weeks later. The 76ers were playing a home game when almost the exact same scenario took place except this time it was right in front of his team's bench. Predictably, the official came up to Jones and asked, "Bobby, did you touch it?"

Jones didn't hesitate when he replied, "Yeah."

Head Coach Billy Cunningham was clearly not happy with his player's display of honesty and stamped his feet in protest. "Bobby! That's his job! Let him make the call!"

Jones didn't respond. A different thought crossed his mind this time.

My integrity's not worth a possession.[2]

Earlier in his NBA career, Jones played for the Denver Nuggets and head coach Larry Brown, who humorously commented that, "Watching Bobby Jones on the basketball court is like watching an honest man in a liars' poker game."[3]

Jones didn't mind his coach's brief fits or the quirky analogies that were inevitably concocted. He was more concerned about living by biblical principles such as the one found in Proverbs 19:1. "Better a poor man who lives with integrity than someone who has deceitful lips and is a fool," King Solomon wisely wrote.

Ironically, Jones didn't become a Christian until his senior year in college, but the seeds of strong, moral character had been planted and watered much earlier. He first learned about integrity from the example of his father Bob, who had played college basketball at the University of Oklahoma. The family moved around a lot when Jones was a boy due to frequent job promotions. But when they landed in Charlotte, North Carolina, his father decided it was time to settle down once and for all no matter what opportunities might come his way. As an 11-year old boy, Jones took notice of his father's act of integrity.[4]

Later in life, Jones was influenced by the integrity of his legendary college basketball coach Dean Smith. He recalls how Smith called each of his players into his office and asked them how they'd like to be coached—corrective and gentle or firm and forceful. Whatever that player requested is exactly how Smith treated that player for the next four years.[5]

After his sophomore season, Jones received a happenstance opportunity to try out for the 1972 Olympic team. After some players became ill, his late entry earned him a spot on the squad. Hosted by Munich, Germany, the usually celebratory event took on a somber tone when terrorists kidnapped 11 Israeli athletes and coaches and ultimately took their lives. Jones says many assumed that the basketball tournament would be cancelled, but it was not. The Americans advanced to the gold medal game against the Soviet Union where Jones and his teammates experienced a sour ending to its Olympic experience.[6]

"Doug Collins hit two free throws to put us up by one with three seconds left," Jones recounts. "They were given three opportunities to inbound the ball. The first two times they failed to score. The third time they did succeed in scoring and they were awarded the gold medal. Interestingly enough, the head of FIBA had been sitting in the stands and he came down and sat at the scorer's table towards the end of the game. He overruled the officials and told them what to do."[7]

The US team collectively decided not to accept the silver medal. It's a decision that Jones still stands by and believes was correct. The team's act of solidarity stood in the face of a blatant lack of integrity, something by which Jones was especially bothered.

"That was really an eye opener for most of us," he says. "We realized it wasn't about sports. It was about big business. It gave us a cynical outlook from that perspective."[8]

It was about a year later when Jones accepted Christ and

slowly began to connect the concept of integrity with the Word of God and the Christian walk. Bible passages such as Proverbs 12:22 rang true with what he already believed in his heart: "Lying lips are detestable to the LORD, but faithful people are His delight."

After Jones' All-American senior season at North Carolina, the Houston Rockets selected him with the fifth overall pick in the 1974 NBA draft. The Carolina Cougars had previously taken Jones in a supplemental draft for the American Basketball Association (ABA) but he opted to go back to school instead of bolting early for a professional career. So when Larry Brown left Carolina (who relocated to St. Louis) for the Denver Nuggets, the head coach was desperate to acquire Jones' services. Jones felt like he had a better chance to play early and often with the Nuggets and decided to play for Brown in the ABA.[9]

Just two years later, the historic NBA-ABA merger took place. Jones had no problem adjusting to the new level of competition and led the Nuggets to a Midwest division title. Because of his burgeoning faith and a life-long commitment to integrity, he also found the off-court challenges that many pro athletes face relatively easy to navigate.

"The toughest thing for me was that we traveled so much and played so many Sunday games that church was irregular," Jones says. "When I was with the 76ers, one good thing that happened was that my pastor would meet with me every Tuesday and that sort of became my church service and Bible study time."[10]

Jones also found accountability early on with Nuggets teammate Claude Terry. He was a veteran player who had played his college ball at Stanford. Terry took Jones under his wing and the two became roommates and close friends as a mentoring relationship developed. But by this time in his career, Terry was no longer a key factor during most games. Usually one of the last players off the bench, he was routinely ridiculed for his faith by other team members. Jones, on the other hand, was a starter and never dealt with the same level of scrutiny.

"We had the same faith," he says. "We were both Christians and we both went to the same church. But what I figured out was that they wouldn't ridicule me because I could block their shot or I could take the ball away from them. So in their eyes, I had that worldly success that prevented them from using my faith as a weakness of mine. I made it a point to be very aggressive in my play—especially defensively. That goes back to my pre-Christian days when I viewed most Christians as weaklings or non-aggressive. I didn't want to be like that."[11]

Jones understood that God had given him a platform for his faith, but he also had begun to realize that part of integrity was giving his best at all times. And just as much as his honesty impacted those around him, so did his relentless pursuit of excellence. When the two concepts came together, it meant playing hard every night and doing so within the context of the rules—even those rules that might potentially be stretched or bent for one's advantage.

"Sometimes if you chop a guy's arm, it's not called a foul," Jones says. "Other nights you can't do that because it *is* called a foul. In the NBA, you play so many games that you almost get to know the officials. You scout them just like you scout your opponents. So you know how it's going to be called and you try to play according to the officials that are on the court at that time. But I never got caught up in trying to sell the call to the officials. I always looked at that as kind of cheesy and a little bit cheap. I also wanted to be a

witness to the officials and to my opponents. That doesn't mean I
was a saint out there. If I got hit in the head, I might have reacted.
I may have thrown an elbow. We're all human. We all do things we
don't want to do. And I'm the same way. I'm human too."[12]

When Jones speaks to churches, sports organizations and
youth groups, he often shares stories like the ones at the beginning
of this chapter. After talking to some young athletes at a camp, an
NBA referee in attendance came to him and made a surprising
claim. There were only a handful of current players he could trust
to help him make the right call.

"In his mind, there were only five guys in the NBA with
integrity," Jones says. "Truthfully, though, there are some solid
Christian guys in the NBA and then there are some young guys
that are believers and they're trying to figure out what they should
do. It's very hard because they want to survive in the league. They
want to make it. But where do they go? Where do they turn? My
prayer for those people is that they would not choose second best.
Most of the time we choose what's second best. We choose the
world's way."[13]

Jones' assertion lines up with a powerful passage of the
Gospel spoken by Jesus in Matthew 7:13-14. "Enter through the
narrow gate. For the gate is wide and the road is broad that leads
to destruction, and there are many who go through it. How narrow
is the gate and difficult the road that leads to life, and few find it."

It isn't easy to do what is right in God's eyes when it seems
as if the vast majority is making a mockery of biblically inspired
moral values. Why make the hard choices when it's so much easier to selfishly feed our fleshly desires? Lying, cheating, stealing, lust-
ing, coveting, gossiping, slacking, boasting and hating are com-

monplace activities in today's world. And there are plenty of willing accomplices in the media and entertainment industries egging
humanity on down the fast track to destruction.

God knows all about the condition of man's heart. That's
why He sent His son Jesus to die for our sins and transform our
lives. The Apostle Paul was a living example of God's powerful plan
and wrote about it to the church in Corinth. "Therefore, if anyone
is in Christ, he is a new creation; old things have passed away, and
look, new things have come." (2 Corinthians 5:17)

When we make the decision to take the narrow road, God
blesses that choice with honor, protection, peace of mind and favor.
"The one who lives with integrity lives securely, but whoever per-
verts his ways will be found out," Solomon writes in Proverbs 10:9.
In the next chapter, he reminds us that, "The one who loves a pure
heart and gracious lips—the king is his friend." We also hear from
David on the subject in Psalm 41:12: "By this I know that You
delight in me: my enemy does not shout in triumph over me. You
supported me because of my integrity and set me in Your presence
forever."

Of course, understanding the benefits of living with godly
integrity doesn't automatically translate into a life that pleases Him.
And as mentioned before, the road to God's Kingdom is straight,
narrow and often difficult to walk when faced with outside influences and our own inner desires that war against us.

That's why God sent the Holy Spirit to dwell the earth and
to indwell those who accept His Son as their Savior. In John 16,
Jesus foretold of this event while explaining to His disciples what
was about to happen (His betrayal, trial, torture, crucifixion and resurrection). The disciples were distraught when they heard these

things, especially the notion that Jesus would leave the earth after being raised from the dead. "It is for your benefit that I go away," He assured them, "because if I don't go away the Counselor will not come to you. If I go, I will send Him to you." (John 16:7)

Jesus went on to explain how the Spirit would "convict the world about sin" (John 16:8) and guide them "into all the truth." (John 16:13) He knew that the only way His people would survive the challenges that lie ahead was by the strength, power, comfort and direction of the Spirit. And the same is true today.

Bobby Jones can certainly attest to that fact.

"Once you decide to live with integrity, the Lord gives you the power of the Holy Spirit," Jones says. "It becomes a habit to where you don't think about it anymore. You just do it. There's not a conflict. You don't worry about it because you know the Lord is going to take care of the situation no matter what."[14]

The Extra Mile

1. What is your definition of the word "integrity?"

2. Have you ever done the right thing and the outcome was in your favor? Have you ever done the right thing and the outcome didn't turn out so well?

3. Do you have people in your life that help you make right choices? Can you tell a difference between times you have friends that keep you accountable as opposed to times when you seem to be going it alone?

4. Why do you think the wide road is so well populated? What are some things on that wide road that have seemed appealing to you?

5. What are some of the benefits you've personally experienced because of integrity?

6. What are some things that you can do today to begin living with more integrity?

Find more of what the Bible says about honesty and integrity by reading these passages: Genesis 37-47, Psalm 24:3-5, Proverbs 4:25-27, Proverbs 28:6, Acts 24:16, 1 Corinthians 15:33, Ephesians 5:1-21, Colossians 3:9-10, Titus 2:1-7 and 1 Peter 3:14-16.

CHAPTER FIFTEEN

Find Your True Identity
Featuring Kelly Clark, USA
Olympic Gold Medalist, Snowboarding

Kelly Clark calls it "the fall heard around the world."[1]

She's joking, but within the snowboarding community it felt that melodramatic when a hard spill took her out of contention for the halfpipe gold medal at the 2006 Winter Olympics in Torino. If Clark had taken a similar tumble four years earlier at the 2002 Winter Olympics in Salt Lake City, she admits it would have been devastating. Instead, the defending halfpipe gold medalist experienced an overwhelming measure of peace amid the disappointment.

"Just two years earlier, my identity was in snowboarding," she explains. "That's how people knew me and that's how I knew myself. That's where I got a lot of my self-worth. But that began to shift and I started to understand that I didn't get my worth from people or from the things that I did."[2]

It's hard to blame Clark for being consumed by snowboarding. She's been doing it since she was seven years old in a hometown called Mount Snow, Vermont, no less. Clark discovered the half pipe when a pipe dragon was installed on the mountain. As a teenager, her love for the sport intensified even though she also found time to give soccer, tennis and surfing a try.

Clark's desire to compete internationally continued to intensify. At the age of 14, she started competing while attending Mount Snow Academy. After two years of local events, she went to the junior USA team camp. With the 1997 introduction of the Winter X-Games and the addition of snowboarding to the Winter Olympics in 1998, Clark now had a greater purpose for pursuing the sport as a career path.

But first, she had to convince her father that snowboarding fulltime was even sustainable. After high school, Clark took a year to prove her belief in such a possibility. By early 2002, there was no longer a need to convince anyone. She dominated that season's X-Games Tour and won the 2002 U.S. Snowboarding Grand Prix.

Nothing, however, could solidify her newfound place among the best than a career-defining moment at the 2002 Winter Olympics in Salt Lake City where Clark secured the first gold medal of those Games for Team USA. Clark's success in 2002 solidified something else that wasn't quite as positive. Snowboarding had become her identity. Not only did Clark rely on the sport for emotional support and personal validation, she truly needed snowboarding to sustain her very existence.

"Snowboarding was everything that I knew," Clark admits. "That's what I did and I poured everything I had into it. I had achieved everything I wanted to do. All of the experiences were incredible and I wouldn't trade them for the world, but it wasn't fulfilling me."[3]

Clark says she "went through the motions"[4] for the next couple of years, but over time began to realize she was looking for something more. In December of 2004 at the first event of the season, the 20-year old contemplated quitting snowboarding altogether. That's when she overheard a conversation and in particular one short, but powerful phrase.

"Two girls were talking and one said to the other, 'God still loves you,'" Clark recalls. "I had never really thought about God before, but those words were undeniably stirring something up in me and I couldn't ignore it."[5]

Clark went back to her hotel room and looked for a Bible. Once she found one she didn't know where to start. So Clark tracked down the girl that had spoken those challenging words—someone she barely knew—and began asking her deep questions about God.

"I thought being a Christian was about following rules and going to church and being good all the time," Clark says. "But she helped me understand that it's about having a relationship with God and not about being religious."[6]

Eventually, Clark learned something else about being a Christian. She was never meant to have her identity wrapped up in snowboarding. Certainly God blessed her with those talents and He ultimately gave them to her for a purpose, but instead of using the sport to glorify Him, she had been using her success as a means for self-fulfillment. Thanks to her providential encounter, Clark now knew better. She was created to be a child of God and to be identified by her relationship with Christ.

The same is true for everyone. And like Clark once did, most people struggle with this concept of identity. It probably isn't snowboarding for most of us, but we can easily be trapped in an identity crisis where things like money, material possessions, talents, athletic abilities, physical attributes, education and even our children or spiritual pursuits like giving or traditional ministry become the centerpiece of our lives. If we're not careful, we will covet the praise and adoration of others based on those things rather than seek to use them as a platform for God's glory and purpose.

When Clark accepted Christ, she experienced the truth found in Galatians 2:20: "For through the law I have died to the law, that I might live to God. I have been crucified with Christ; and I no longer live, but Christ lives in me. The life I now live in the flesh, I live by faith in the Son of God, who loved me and gave Himself for me."

It's a miraculous thing that takes place when we believe in Him and ask Him to cleanse us of our sins. We are transformed into a new person or "new creation" as Paul refers to it in 2 Corinthians 5:17. That means our life is no longer about pleasing ourselves or living in pursuit of our dreams. When Christ comes to live in us, we are now vessels of His love, His virtues, His forgiveness and His agenda. And while this may seem to be a daunting responsibility, the beautiful truth is that we can rely on His strength to help us achieve the purpose that He has placed within us.

We also can withstand whatever attacks might come our way. Romans 8:36 confirms that, because of our relationship with Christ, "we are being put to death all day long; we are counted as sheep to be slaughtered." Even so, Romans 8:37 then reminds us that, "in all these things we are more than victorious through Him who loved us."

For Clark, that realization gave her the freedom to be whom she was called to be—an elite international snowboarder with a platform from which she might share the Gospel of hope with all who will listen. That also meant she didn't have to worry about winning and losing anymore. It didn't mean she would stop working hard and diligently commit herself to perfecting her abilities. But when she didn't win, and even in those times she experienced severe disappointment (like at the 2006 Olympics), it wouldn't be the end of the world.

"There's no place where you can get freedom apart from Him," Clark says. "I've brought that freedom into my snowboarding. It really does set me apart from a lot of the athletes. I get to do what I love with the One that I love."[7]

The Extra Mile

1. What are some material things, accomplishments, talents, etc., by which people can often be identified?

2. Does anything from that list resonate with you? If not, what you would say is the one thing that most defines who you are?

3. Can you think of a time when you experienced great disappointment due to a personal failure or because you fell short of a goal or dream? Was it difficult to bounce back? Explain why or why not.

4. What does it personally mean to have your identity in Christ? Is that something you've been able to experience or is it something with which you've struggled at times? Explain.

5. How would you describe the difference you feel in times when your identity has been wrapped up in personal things as opposed to times when you understood that your identity was in Christ?

6. What are some daily reminders that might help you keep a bet-

ter perspective when it comes to your spiritual identity?

Find more of what the Bible says about what it means to have your identity in Christ by reading these passages: Romans 6:6, Romans 5:10, Romans 8:15-16, Galatians 3:29 and John 15:15.

CHAPTER SIXTEEN

Strive for Humility
Featuring Kevin Durant, USA
Olympic Athlete, Basketball

It's official. The word "rising" can now be taken out of the mix. Kevin Durant is a bona fide NBA star. As the leader of the Oklahoma City Thunder and perennial scoring champion, there's no doubt that the hard-working Durant will be making waves for years to come.

But what most people don't know is that Durant is equally committed to improving his walk with God. His faith in Christ has been instilled in his heart for many years now thanks to committed family members back home.

"I was always intrigued simply about how we got here," Durant says. "Why do we do the things we do? Who made us like this? My mom always sat me down and talked to me and now I have spiritual teachers that help me out."[1]

While Durant has taken the slow and steady approach to his faith journey, the NBA All-Star's path to fame and fortune has been more akin to a spaceship launch. He made some serious rumblings at the youth league and AAU levels before a quick stop at the University of Texas where as a freshman in 2007 he won the John R. Wooden Award and was named Naismith College Player of the Year.[2]

When Durant unsurprisingly left for the NBA draft after just one collegiate season, he was selected second overall by the Seattle SuperSonics. That year, he averaged 20.3 points per game and ran away with the NBA Rookie of the Year Award.[3] The next season, Durant moved along with the franchise to Oklahoma City where the renamed Thunder became an instant hit. The fans quickly embraced Durant despite having ties to the Sooner State's archenemy Longhorns.

And as much as Durant has enjoyed playing for Texas and now the Thunder, there's nothing like the feeling he experienced when he first donned the red, white and blue as a member of the USA Basketball Men's National Team at the 2010 FIFA World Championship in Turkey.

"It was an unbelievable feeling; first of all, to play for your country, and to represent your country and your family, and the city and the state that you come from," Durant says. "Words can't explain how excited I was when the gold medal game was over and we'd won. It felt like we'd won the NBA championship. It was a great feeling to represent everyone back here in the USA and to come together with that group of guys and do something that nobody thought we could do with the team we had."[4]

Some might look at Durant and cite natural talent and ability as the key to his success. Certainly, no one will argue that the 6'9" forward isn't blessed with some easily recognizable God-given gifts. But there's another element at play that has pushed Durant into an elite level alongside superstars such as Kobe Bryant, LeBron James, Dwight Howard and Chris Paul—hard work.

Oklahoma City Thunder television broadcaster Brian Davis can certainly attest to that unrelenting part of Durant's basketball life.

"During Kevin's rookie season, we were on the road in Minnesota and the hotel in Minneapolis had an athletic club on its third floor," Davis says. "It was late and the club was about to close so some of the coaches ran down there to get in a quick workout. There was hardly anybody in there. All of the sudden they heard a ball bouncing. There was a basketball court around the corner. They went over there to see who was bouncing the ball and it was Kevin. Even after flying into town so late, he wanted to get some shots up. That's just what he does."[5]

Durant's notable work ethic isn't just driven by a deep-seeded desire to score points, win games and earn healthy contracts. In fact, those close to him would argue there's something else at play. As it turns out, Durant is somewhat the anti-star. Sure, he enjoys himself on the court and he has plenty of fun away from the game. But unlike so many contemporaries that get caught up in the hype of their own fame, Durant has exemplified a rare measure of humility.

That's not to say it's been an easy road.

"It's tough man. I can't lie. I can't lie about that," Durant candidly admits. "But I always kind of pinch myself and say that any day this can be gone. In the Bible, the Lord exalts humility and that's one thing I try to have all the time. When I'm in front of people, when I'm talking to people or when people tell me I'm great, I (remind myself that I) can always be better. I always work on what I have now."[6]

Durant's paraphrased reference to Matthew 23:12 is certainly exceptional in professional sports these days. In that passage, Jesus told his followers, "Whoever exalts himself will be humbled, and whoever humbles himself will be exalted." Thankfully for Durant, he has always had sufficient help keeping his ego in check.

"I know that if I try to get a big head, my mom is going to

do a great job of bringing me back down to size," Durant laughs. "I have the best of both worlds with the coaches we have here and my parents and my family doing it back at home. I'm in pretty good hands."[7]

Durant's bent towards humility is something Davis has noticed from day one.

"It's just the way he's wired," he says. "If you look at Kevin's background, his mom was a police officer for the postal service. His dad was a jail guard in Montgomery County, Maryland. He's got law enforcement and discipline in his background. I've been around his family a little bit including both of his grandmothers. The young man has obviously been raised in a very loving and caring environment. That counts for an awful lot."[8]

Because of his spiritual upbringing, Durant was quick to follow the example of teammates who attended chapel services before each game. Former teammate Kevin Ollie provided such leadership until his retirement in 2010. At that point, Durant humbled himself, moved out of his comfort zone, and took on the responsibility of rounding up players for pre-game devotion.

In the Bible, there are many examples of humility, but the Book of Exodus tells us about a man named Moses who was later described as "a very humble man, more so than any man on the face of the earth." (Number 12:3)

After escaping death as a child (Exodus 2:1-10) and later as a young man (Exodus 2:11-15), the Hebrew-born Moses went from living the lavish lifestyle of a prince to tending sheep in the land then known as Midian (Exodus 3:1). After 40 anonymous years, Moses was jarred out of his mediocre life when God spoke to him through a burning bush (Exodus 3:2-9). It was time for Moses to go back to Egypt and lead his people out of captivity.

Once the adopted son of royalty, Moses now felt weak and powerless to accomplish such a seemingly impossible task. "Who am I that I should go to Pharaoh and that I should bring the Israelites out of Egypt?" Moses asked. (Exodus 3:11)

God answered, "I will certainly be with you." (Exodus 3:12)

Because Moses obeyed God, He was endued with great power and authority. Through him, God performed many miracles and freed the Hebrews from captivity. But it would not have happened if Moses had not humbly submitted to the Lord and recognized that his newfound leadership gifts were from God.

There is no greater example of humility, however, than in the life of Christ. And there's no better way to describe how He displayed that humility than in Philippians 2:5-8. In that passage, Paul writes, "Make your own attitude that of Christ Jesus, who, existing in the form of God, did not consider equality with God as something to be used for His own advantage. Instead He emptied Himself by assuming the form of a slave, taking on the likeness of men. And when He had come as a man in His external form, He humbled Himself by becoming obedient to the point of death—even to death on a cross."

When Jesus came to earth, His birth and subsequent life took place in the most humbling and undesirable of circumstances. Even during His ministry, when He was followed by the masses and revered for His teachings and miracles, Jesus was poor and reviled by the self-important religious leaders. And His public, humiliating death took place on a cross—a punishment reserved for society's most egregious criminals.

If He humbled Himself in order to bring us the Gospel of eternal life through salvation, how much more should we put aside our pride and live with humility as a testimony of love and service to those around us.

In John 3:27, John the Baptist best described this reality when told his disciples "No one can receive a single thing unless it's given to him from heaven. Later in verse 30, the prophet spoke these powerful but challenging words: "He must increase, but I must decrease."

It goes against our very human nature to acknowledge God as the provider of all gifts. It's even more difficult to resist our selfish desires in an effort to set Him front and center on the stage of our life. Durant understands that ugly truth and knows it's only possible to pursue humility when you have a heart of gratitude.

"I've just got to be thankful to the Lord for the gifts He's given me," Durant says. "My gift back to Him is to always be humble and to always try to work as hard as I can. I've got to continue to be that way."[9]

The Extra Mile

1. What are some areas of your life where you struggle with pride?

2. Have you ever had a situation where you were knocked off your pedestal and you took a shot to your pride or your ego? How did that humble you?

3. Why do you think it's so hard for humans to live with humility?

4. What are some of your talents and abilities? Do you generally think of them as God-given or man-made?

5. What are some ways that you can begin striving for humility today? How do you think living a more humble life might change your circumstances or impact the people around you?

Find more of what the Bible says about humility by reading these passages: Luke 18:9-14, 2 Corinthians 11:30, Ephesians 2:8-9, 1 Peter 5:5-7 and James 4:6-10.

CHAPTER SEVENTEEN

Stay Focused
Featuring Laura Wilkinson, USA
Olympic Gold Medalist, Diving

It really doesn't matter what sport we're talking about: it takes incredible focus in order to become an elite international athlete. Whether it's in training or during the actual competition, fighting through distractions and keeping an eye on the prize is essential to the Olympian's success.

Take diving, for instance. Laura Wilkinson can attest to the single-minded attention to detail required to jump from a 10-meter platform, perform an acrobatic stunt while careening towards the pool, and then hit the water with maximum precision and minimal splash.

"When I trained for a competition, I was completely focused," Wilkinson says. "I spent hours upon hours every day. I thought outside the box on how to make myself better. I studied videos. I talked to people about it. I poured my life into it."[1]

During the height of her career, Wilkinson's passion for diving was fueled by a pure love for the sport and the adrenaline that accompanies it. But make no mistake about it, Wilkinson was also driven by the loftiest of goals.

"When I competed, I had one ultimate dream, to win gold," Wilkinson says. "So I did what it took to win. I trained my body in a specific way to be the strongest, quickest and most explosive. I practiced every day for hours on end, perfecting all the little details that go into a great performance. And I went into the competition with my focus on those things I had been practicing and how to do them all to my very best ability."[2]

But what happens when distractions come along or, worse, a major crisis that seeks to derail those hopes and dreams? Wilkinson found out that serious bumps in the road could either break her concentration or sharpen her focus. Just three months before the US Trials, Wilkinson suffered three broken metatarsals in her right foot. She admits that even prior to the injury, her focus was waning. Initially, Wilkinson questioned the circumstance and even wondered if she'd made the right decision to quit school and aim squarely at her first Olympic appearance.

"I knew it might be my one and only chance," Wilkinson says. "I was going to give it all I had. When I broke my foot, it was this big letdown for about a week and then I realized how bad I wanted to be back in the water. I just kind of made up mind that I was going for it and I wasn't going to look back. I just knew that God had given me this dream, so I had to do it."[3]

While recovering from surgery, she refocused on her goal. Wilkinson would hop up the ladder and sit on the edge of the platform while visualizing her dives and even doing the arm motions for each jump. She watched hours of video and paid closer attention to the mental side of her craft. Although her foot wasn't fully healed in time for competition, she fought through the pain and took solace in the fact that she would be landing hands first in the water. Wilkinson's steely resolve and sharpened focus led to a dominating 40-point victory at the US Trials just three weeks after she had gotten back into the water. From there, she went to Sydney and claimed an upset gold medal victory over the favorites from China.[4]

Wilkinson's focus paved the way for the rest of her career

that ended with three Olympic appearances (2000, 2004 and 2008) plus gold medal performances at the 2005 World Championships, the 2004 World Cup and the 1998 Goodwill Games—something that no other female diver had previously accomplished. That opened the door to her current life as a motivational speaker, broadcast commentator and diving instructor. Wilkinson also employs a great deal of focus when balancing those responsibilities with her most cherished roles as a mother and wife.[5]

Perhaps that's why she can relate so well to the story of Peter found in Matthew 14:22-33. In that passage, we read about a night when the disciples traveled from one shore to another by boat. Jesus stayed behind. Having traveled a mile ahead, the disciples suddenly faced a massive storm that brought with it intense winds and crashing waves.

That's when the frightened men heard a voice. It was Jesus who had walked on the water to their boat. The disciples feared that it was a ghost, so Jesus called to them and said, "Have courage! It is I. Don't be afraid." (Matthew 14:27)

To no one's surprise, Peter was the first to respond. "Lord, if it's You, command me to come to You on the water." (Matthew 14:28) Upon Jesus' instruction, the bold and often brash disciple got out of the boat and walked on the water toward Him. Peter had spent months around the Son of God. He had seen the miracles. He had heard the revolutionary teachings. In that moment, Peter was emboldened to bravely obey the Lord.

"If you think about it, it took an incredible amount of faith for Peter to walk out to Jesus in the first place," Wilkinson says. "It's the middle of the night, pitch black, the wind is raging. But Peter in his beautiful child-like faith wants to just jump right out of the boat and go meet Jesus on the water."[6]

But when given the opportunity to trust Jesus, Peter "saw the strength of the wind" and "was afraid." (Matthew 14:30) He essentially took his eyes of the Lord and became distracted by the frightening circumstance in which he found himself. But, "Immediately Jesus reached out His hand, caught hold of (Peter), and said to him, 'You of little faith, why did you doubt?'"

It could be argued that Peter's near death experience was the turning point in his life. After this event, we see a more focused disciple who starts to truly see Jesus for who He is and begin to understand more deeply the lessons he had been learning. It's not to say that Peter was perfect. He certainly made his share of mistakes along the way (e.g., see Mark 14:66-72). Wilkinson had a similar experience when her seemingly devastating injury turned into a rallying point for a refocused approach to winning the gold medal.

Still, it's amazing how our faith can be so easily shaken. We can have the intense focus of an Olympic athlete one day and then in an instant find ourselves drowning like Peter did that night. But there's something we can do to retain our focus, even amid the most troublesome situations. In Colossians 3:2, the Apostle Paul writes, "Set your mind on what is above, not on what is on the earth."

That might sound contradictory to Wilkinson's earthly goal of winning a gold medal, but it really isn't. In fact, the Lord placed those goals inside her spirit. There was no guarantee that she would win at the 2000 Sydney Games, but Wilkinson knew that it was her calling at the time to pursue diving with excellence and give God the glory no matter what the result. When we focus on God and His ways, we will find ourselves in the center of His plan for our lives. As long as we don't allow distractions and disappointments to break that focus, we will be empowered to, in a sense, walk on water with Jesus and fulfill whatever calling He has placed on our lives.

Just like her time as an elite athlete, Wilkinson knows that people continue to watch what she says and what she does. She understands her purpose now better than ever—to be an example for her family, her friends and anyone she has the opportunity to influence because of her Olympic platform. And that, no doubt, requires the same kind of intense focus as it took to fight through an injury and win the gold.

"I need to keep my eyes and heart focused on Jesus no matter how crazy and frightening the world around me may look and feel," Wilkinson says. "And whatever bright ideas or goals I come up with, I need to first seek out what God wants me doing and where He's driving me. Because on my own, I'm going nowhere fast."[7]

The Extra Mile

1. What does it mean to you to be focused? In what areas of your life is focus important?

2. Do you ever struggle with focus? Explain.

3. How can you relate to either Laura Wilkinson or Peter's stories?

4. What are some of the things that often distract you from staying focused on God's calling for your life?

5. What do you think it means to "set your eyes on what is above?"

6. What are some things you can start doing today that will improve your focus and keep you on the path that God has laid before you?

Find more of what the Bible says about staying focused by reading these passages: Psalm 119:15, Matthew 14:22-33, Matthew 25:1-13, Romans 8:5 and Philippians 4:6-8.

CHAPTER EIGHTEEN

Finish the Race
Featuring Ryan Hall, USA
Olympic Athlete, Marathon

Marathon runners are trained for endurance. They fight through every kind of pain imaginable in order to finish a grueling 26.2-mile race. Maybe that's what makes Ryan Hall's candid admission so remarkable. The fastest American marathoner almost quit.

Hall wasn't running marathons at the time, but he already had the skill set of a long-distance runner having successfully competed at a high level in cross country and track and field as a highly-touted prep athlete and early in his career at Stanford.

But during his sophomore year, injuries and sub-par performances frustrated Hall so much that he dropped out of school for the winter quarter.

"I was really struggling with everything at the time," Hall admits. "I was struggling with my grades, with adjusting to college life and with running. I felt like a failure in almost every way."[1]

During his relatively young but heralded career, Hall has dealt with injuries, coaching changes and disappointing performances, yet he says the mental, emotional and spiritual anguish attached to such a difficult question of purpose is the most difficult circumstance he's been forced to overcome during his journey an elite international competitor.

"I was struggling with my identity and how I saw myself," Hall says. "I viewed myself based on my results and I was really depressed because I was failing. When I went home, I had to figure out who I was and how God saw me. I had to break away from the performance-based mentality that had been the driving force in my life to that point."[2]

Hall was also reminded of something that had happened about six years earlier. One day, at the age of 14, he was suddenly inspired to run around the lake in his hometown of Big Bear City, California. It was almost as if God had whispered the thought into his ear, Hall explains "From that moment, he believed he was made to be a runner and he embraced the athletic discipline as a calling.

"That vision has enabled me to not give up," Hall says. "I knew from day one, because God told me this, that I was going to one day run with the best runners in the world and I would be given this gift to help other people. Today, I am finally starting to walk in fulfillment of this dream, but it wasn't easy getting here. There were a lot of times along the way that I felt like quitting, but I knew I hadn't yet accomplished what God had told me I was going to do. So I had to keep going."[3]

Hall also credits a host of supportive family members and friends who have encouraged him through "many hard times" that he expected would come with the territory. He has also been buoyed by the realization that running isn't about winning races.

"It's not my job to accomplish great things," Hall says. "It's my job to stay close to God and to simply be all that He has created me to be. If I do that, then the results will be exactly what they are supposed to be and I will accomplish God's mission for my life."[4]

Over time, Hall began to learn what it took to be an elite international competitor. He started to see a common thread among Olympians such as determination, hard work, talent and that aforementioned group of supporters. Hall also discovered that there are some individual qualities that vary from one athlete to the next.

"For me, it has taken an incredible amount of resilience," he says. "I have had to get back up after falling down over and over and over again in my career. There have been many more challenging races and disappointments than successes."[5]

In fact, Hall believes that the manner in which an athlete handles failure is what ultimately determines the character and mettle of an Olympian. That's why Proverbs 24:16 is one of his favorite Bible verses. "Though a righteous man falls seven times, he will get up," King Solomon declares.

"God always has given me the grace and strength to get back up after I have fallen," Hall says. "I have found that He has given me everything I need to accomplish what He has created me to be and called me to do."[6]

Sometimes, Hall has briefly forgotten this truth during the course of a tough race. At the 2008 Summer Games in Beijing, he was fulfilling a lifelong dream of running in the Olympic Stadium, and in his mind, he was emerging from each race triumphant. In reality, he was in 10th place and "not very happy with how things had turned out."[7]

Hall had struggled throughout his training and wasn't having his best race. In his frustration, he had failed to recognize how much he had overcome and the level of endurance it had taken for him to perform as well as he did.

"But at that moment, I felt like God met me in the quiet of the tunnel that led into the stadium," Hall recounts. "He reassured me that even though that moment wasn't everything I had dreamt of, it was everything I needed at that point in my career. Through that circumstance, He was developing my character, which is far more valuable than any Olympic medal because character lasts our entire lives and we are able to build on it for future challenges."[8]

Call it determination. Call is resilience. Call it will power. What Hall has been really talking about is the biblical principle of endurance. Sure, endurance is a physical characteristic that allows individuals to overcome obstacles in their way or outlast extreme circumstances that could very easily stop them in their tracks. But there are emotional and spiritual components to endurance as well.

Perhaps that's why life has often been compared to the marathon. Both are long races with high points, low points and the full spectrum of emotions in between. This is especially true for the follower of Christ who may not only face everyday challenges but also supernatural forces that seek to push them off the narrow road and hinder their relationship with God.

It's shouldn't be surprising to see that analogy used more than once in the Bible. We find a vivid description of such in Hebrews 12:1: "Therefore, since we also have such a large cloud of witnesses surrounding us, let us lay aside every weight and the sin that so easily ensnares us. Let us run with endurance the race that lies before us."

In this instance, the key to endurance is getting rid of anything that slows us down—weights in the form of fear, doubt and uncertainty, or sins such as pride, greed and selfishness. It also means ridding our minds of past failures and looking ahead to the blessed future that we have been promised.

In Philippians 3:13-14, the Apostle Paul underscores that truth with these words: "Forgetting what is behind and reaching forward to what is ahead, I pursue as my goal the prize promised by God's heavenly call in Christ Jesus."

That prize is two-fold. Here on earth, our prize is abundant life and joy despite our circumstances. Beyond this existence, our prize is eternal life in Heaven with God and a never-ending joy that will be better than any gold medal, trophy, material possession or cash reward.

Towards the end of his "race," Paul encouraged the church to continue long after his death. His words in 2 Timothy 4:6-8 provide another descriptive comparison to life in the context of an athletic competition and the endurance necessary to prevail:

"For I am already being poured out as a drink offering, and the time for my departure is close. I have fought the good fight, I have finished the race, I have kept the faith. There is reserved for me in the future the crown of righteousness, which the Lord, the righteous Judge, will give me on that day, and not only to me, but to all those who have loved His appearing."

Because of his endurance, Hall has achieved some significant earthly prizes. He has won an NCAA championship, claimed national awards, broken records and raced on the biggest international stages—though nothing compares to the prize he is truly running to win.

But in order to finish the race, Hall, just like all of us, must drop that burdensome baggage mentioned in Hebrews 12:1 by "keeping our eyes on Jesus, the source and perfecter of our faith, who for the joy that lay before Him endured a cross and despised the shame and has sat down at the right hand of God's throne." (Hebrews 12:2)

When Hall is competing, he spends a lot of his time thinking about Jesus on the cross. Vivid images from the film *The Passion of the Christ* often flood his mind. As his feet pound the pavement, he can see the nails being pounded into the Savior's hands and feet. It reminds him that nothing he has endured in training and nothing he must endure during a marathon compares to what Jesus suffered through when He was beaten, whipped, spit upon, cursed at and ultimately hung upon a cross to die so that we might have eternal life.

"I hope that my story leads people into an experience with Jesus," Hall concludes. "I want to inspire people to look to the heavens for strength and to enter into a relationship with the One who has infinite power and love and who created us to love Him and to be loved by Him."[9]

The Extra Mile

1. What do you think of when you hear the word "endurance?"

2. In what areas do you have endurance? In what areas is your endurance lacking?

3. What are some of the weights and sins that slow you down while running this "race" as a follower of Christ?

4. How can keeping your eyes on Jesus help rid you of that baggage?

5. What does it mean to you to "finish the race?"

6. How might reflecting on what Jesus endured on the cross help build up your spiritual endurance?

Find more of what the Bible says about endurance by reading these passages: Romans 5:3-4, Philippians 4:12-13, Galatians 6:9, Hebrews 10:36, Hebrews 12:1-12 and James 1:2-4.

Footnotes

Chapter 1 – Trust God's Plan featuring Dave Johnson

[1] World Burns Club, "To A Mouse," http://www.worldburnsclub.com/poems/translations/554.htm (accessed January 18, 2012).

[2] Dave Johnson, interview with the author, October 25, 2011.

[3] Ibid.

[4] Ibid.

[5] Julie Cart, "Decathlete Dave Johnson May Have Stress Fracture," *Los Angeles Times,* August 1992.

[6] Dave Johnson, interview with the author, October 25, 2011.

[7] Ibid.

[8] Ibid.

[9] Ibid.

[10] Ibid.

[11] Ibid.

[12] Ibid.

[13] World Burns Club, "To A Mouse," http://www.worldburnsclub.com/poems/translations/554.htm (accessed January 18, 2012).

[14] Dave Johnson, interview with the author, October 25, 2011.

Chapter 2 – Keep a Steady Pace featuring Hunter Kemper

[1] Hunter Kemper, interview with the author, January 10, 2012.

[2] Ibid.

[3] HunterKemper.com, "About Hunter," http://www.hunterkemper.com/hunterkemper.com/about_Hunter.html (accessed January 21, 2012).

[4] Ibid.

[5] Hunter Kemper, interview with the author, January 10, 2012.

[6] Ibid.

[7] Ibid.

[8] Ibid.

[9] Ibid.

[10] Ibid.

Chapter 3 – Live For God Not Men featuring Tamika Catchings

[1] Tamika Catchings, interview with the author, March 29, 2010.
[2] Ibid.
[3] Tamika Catchings, interview with the author, August 5, 2011.
[4] Tamika Catchings, interview with the author, March 29, 2010.
[5] Tamika Catchings, interview with the author, April 3, 2008.
[6] Tamika Catchings, interview with the author, March 29, 2010.

Chapter 4 – Get Spiritually Fit featuring Lyndon Rush

[1] Lyndon Rush, interview with the author, October 31, 2011.
[2] Ibid.
[3] Ibid.
[4] Ibid.
[5] Ibid.
[6] Ibid.

Chapter 5 – Put Up a Fight featuring Shannon Miller

[1] Shannon Miller, interview with the author, November 11, 2011.
[2] Ibid.
[3] Ibid.
[4] Ibid.
[5] Ibid.
[6] Ibid.
[7] Ibid.

Chapter 6 – Discipline Your Self featuring Chris Byrd

[1] Chris Byrd, interview with the author, January 8, 2012.
[2] Ibid.
[3] Ibid.
[4] Chris Byrd, interview with the author, March 14, 2008.
[5] Ibid.
[6] Ibid.
[7] Chris Byrd website, "The Ring,"
http://www.chrisbyrdboxing.com/ring.html (accessed January 16, 2012).
[8] Ibid.

[9] Chris Byrd, interview with the author, January 8, 2012.

[10] Ibid.

[11] Ibid.

[12] Chris Byrd, interview with the author, March 14, 2008.

Chapter 7 – Be Faithful With Your Gifts featuring Ruth Riley

[1] Sheryl Swoopes was the first female basketball player to win an NCAA championship, WNBA title and Olympic gold medal. She completed the accomplishment in 1997 when the Houston Comets won the WNBA title. Kara Wolters was the second female athlete to reach this goal when she won an Olympic gold medal in 2000. Swin Cash and Sue Bird joined this list of athletes at the 2004 Olympics along with Ruth Riley. The most recent player to win each of these three titles was Diana Taurasi who added her name to the list when she led the Phoenix Mercury to a WNBA title in 2007.

[2] Ruth Riley, interview with the author, November 18, 2011.

[3] Ibid.

[4] Ibid.

[5] Ibid.

[6] Ibid.

Chapter 8 – Go Against the Grain featuring Jarome Iginla

[1] Jarome Iginla, interview with the author, November 27, 2006.

[2] Chad Bonham, "Breaking the Ice," *New Man,* March/April 2007.

[3] Ibid.

[4] Ibid.

[5] Ibid.

[6] Ibid.

[7] Ibid.

[8] Ibid.

[9] Ibid.

[10] Ibid.

Chapter 9 – Shine Your Light featuring Tobin Heath

[1] US Soccer, Tobin Heath profile, http://www.ussoccer.com/teams/wnt/h/tobin-heath.aspx (accessed January 4, 2012).

[2] Tobin Heath, interview with the author, August 12, 2011.

[3] US Soccer, Tobin Heath profile, http://www.ussoccer.com/teams/wnt/h/tobin-heath.aspx (accessed January 4, 2012).

[4] Tobin Heath, interview with the author, August 12, 2011.

[5] US Soccer, Women's World Cup History, http://www.ussoccer.com/news/womens-national-team/2011/06/womens-world-cup-history.aspx (accessed January 13, 2012).

[6] FIFA.com, 2011 Women's World Cup Results, http://www.fifa.com/womensworldcup/matches/index.html (accessed January 4, 2012).

[7] Ibid.

[8] FIFA.com, "Japan edge USA for maiden title," http://www.fifa.com/womensworldcup/matches/round=255989/match=300144437/summary.html, July 17, 2011.

[9] Tobin Heath, interview with the author, August 12, 2011.

[10] Ibid.

[11] Ibid.

[12] Ibid.

[13] Ibid.

[14] Ibid.

Chapter 10 – Swim Upstream featuring Josh Davis

[1] Josh Davis, interview with the author, November 28, 2007.

[2] Ibid.

[3] Ibid.

[4] Ibid.

[5] Ibid.

[6] Ibid.

[7] Ibid.

[8] Ibid.

[9] Michelle A. Vu, "Iraq soars eight places on list of world's most dangerous countries for Christians," *Christianity Today*, January 6, 2011.

[10] Josh Davis, interview with the author, February 16, 2012.

[11] Ibid.

Chapter 11 – Give Credit Where Credit is Due featuring Chad Hedrick

1 Chad Bonham, "Faith on the Ice and Snow," *Charisma,* February 2010.

2 Chad Hedrick, interview with the author, November 24, 2009.

3 Bonham, "Faith on the Ice and Snow," *Charisma,* February 2010.

4 Chad Hedrick, interview with the author, November 24, 2009.

5 Chad Hedrick, interview with the author, November 24, 2009.

Chapter 12 – Play With Passion featuring DeLisha Milton-Jones

1 DeLisha Milton-Jones, interview with the author, May 29, 2010.

2 Chad Bonham, "D-Nasty Sunshine," *Sharing the Victory,* August/September 2010.

3 Ibid.

4 Camille Wooden, interview with the author, June 2, 2010.

5 Bonham, "D-Nasty Sunshine," *Sharing the Victory,* August/September 2010.

6 Bonham, "D-Nasty Sunshine," *Sharing the Victory,* August/September 2010.

Chapter 13 – Serve It Up featuring Michael Chang

1 Michael Chang, interview with the author, February 29, 2008.

2 Ibid.

3 Jerry Crowe, "Quitting was an option for Michael Chang," Los Angeles Times, http://articles.latimes.com/2009/may/12/sports/sp-crowe12, May 12, 2009.

4 Michael Chang, interview with the author, February 29, 2008.

5 Ibid.

6 Ibid.

7 Ibid.

8 The Chang Family Foundation website, http://www.mchang.com/cff/about.html (accessed January 14, 2012).

9 The Chang Family Foundation website, http://www.mchang.com/cff/sportsleague.html (accessed January 14, 2012).

10 Michael Chang, interview with the author, February 29, 2008.

[11] Ibid.
[12] Ibid.

Chapter 14 – Take the Narrow Road featuring Bobby Jones

[1] Bobby Jones, interview with the author, February 25, 2008.
[2] Ibid.
[3] Reference.com, "Bobby Jones,"
http://www.reference.com/browse/bobby+jones+%28basketball,+bo rn+1951%29 (accessed January 19, 2012).
[4] Bobby Jones, interview with the author, February 25, 2008.
[5] Ibid.
[6] Ibid.
[7] Ibid.
[8] Ibid.
[9] Ibid.
[10] Ibid.
[11] Ibid.
[12] Ibid.
[13] Ibid.
[14] Ibid.

Chapter 15 – Find Your True Identity featuring Kelly Clark

[1] Chad Bonham, "Faith on the Ice and Snow," *Charisma,* February 2010.
[2] Kelly Clark, interview with the author, November 13, 2009.
[3] Ibid.
[4] Ibid.
[5] Ibid.
[6] Ibid.
[7] Bonham, "Faith on the Ice and Snow," *Charisma,* February 2010.

Chapter 16 – Strive for Humility featuring Kevin Durant

[1] Chad Bonham, "Quiet Thunder," *Sports Spectrum,* Spring 2011.
[2] NBA.com, Kevin Durant Player Profile,
http://www.nba.com/playerfile/kevin_durant, (accessed November 21, 2011).
[3] Ibid.

4 Bonham, "Quiet Thunder," *Sports Spectrum,* Spring 2011.

5 Ibid.

6 Ibid.

7 Ibid.

8 Brian Davis, interview with the author, October 12, 2010.

9 Kevin Durant, interview with the author, October 12, 2010.

Chapter 17 – Stay Focused featuring Laura Wilkinson

1 LauraWilkinson.com, "Day 19: Striving For A Crown," http://www.laurawilkinson.com/40%20Day%20Journey/Day19.htm (accessed January 22, 2012).

2 Ibid.

3 Laura Wilkinson, interview with the author, January 17, 2008.

4 Ibid.

5 LauraWilkinson.com, "Laura Wilkinson Bio," http://www.laurawilkinson.com/bio.htm (accessed January 23, 2012).

6 LauraWilkinson.com, "Day 7: Walking On Water," http://www.laurawilkinson.com/40%20Day%20Journey/Day7.htm (accessed January 22, 2012).

7 Ibid.

Chapter 18 – Finish the Race featuring Ryan Hall

1 Ryan Hall, interview with the author, December 29, 2011.

2 Ibid.

3 Ibid.

4 Ibid.

5 Ibid.

6 Ibid.

7 Ibid.

8 Ibid.

9 Ibid.

Affiliated Charities, Ministries and Organizations

100 Black Men of American, Inc.
www.100blackmen.org

Association of Baptists for World Evangelism
www.abwe.org

Canadian National Sport Chaplaincy
c/o Steve Sellers
100 Convention Way
Cochrane, AB T4C 2G2

Catch The Stars Foundation
www.catchthestars.org

Chad Hedrick Foundation
www.chadhedrickfoundation.com

Chang Family Foundation
http://mchang.com

Corban University Athletics
www.gowarriorsgo.com

Kelly Clark Foundation
http://kellyclarkfoundation.org

Laura Wilkinson Foundation
www.lfound.org

Shannon Miller Foundation
www.shannonmillerfoundation.com

The Steps Foundation
http://thestepsfoundation.org

Triad Trust
http://triadtrust.org

Contact
Information

Chris Byrd
www.chrisbyrdboxing.com
www.chrisbyrdspeaks.com

Tamika Catchings
www.catchin24.com
Twitter @Catchin24

Michael Chang
http://changtennis.com

Kelly Clark
Twitter @Kellyclarkfdn

Josh Davis
www.joshdavis.com
Twitter @JoshDavis_USA

Kevin Durant
www.kevindurant35.com
Twitter @KDTrey5

Ryan Hall
Twitter @ryanhall3

Tobin Heath
Twitter @TobinHeath

Chad Hedrick
www.chadhedrick.com
Twitter @chadhedrick

Dave Johnson
http://facebook.com/decadave

DeLisha Milton-Jones
Twitter @DelishaMJones

Hunter Kemper
www.hunterkemper.com
Twitter @hunterkemper

Shannon Miller
www.shannonmillerlifestyle.com
www.facebook.com/SMLifestyle
Twitter @SMillerGold

Ruth Riley
www.ruthriley.com

Lyndon Rush
Twitter @Goldrush781

Laura Wilkinson
www.laurawilkinson.com
Twitter @Lala_the_diver